CREATING WITH CARD WEAVING

A Simple, Non-Loom Technique

Sally Specht

and

Sandra Rawlings

CROWN PUBLISHERS, INC., NEW YORK

Title page: shoulder bag by Robert Cranford.
(Photo, Bob Warner)

Inquiries should be addressed to Crown Publishers, Inc.,
419 Park Avenue South, New York, N.Y. 10016.

Library of Congress Catalog Card Number: 72-96647
ISBN: 0-517-503484
ISBN: 0-517-503794
Printed in the United States of America
Published simultaneously in Canada by
General Publishing Company Limited

Design by Nedda Balter

CONTENTS

ACKNOWLEDGMENTS

The authors wish to acknowledge the significant contribution made by the many card weavers throughout the country who permitted their creations to be photographed and published. All photographs, unless otherwise noted, are by Rickie Wong and Andrew Weber whose help and devotion to this project were extraordinary. To list the many friends and relatives who assisted would consume so much space as to challenge the publishers. Nevertheless these people made the work possible, some by active participation others by exercising exceptional patience. The authors feel a great debt of gratitude to them all.

Sally Specht
Sandra Rawlings

Note: All weavings by Sally Specht unless otherwise credited.

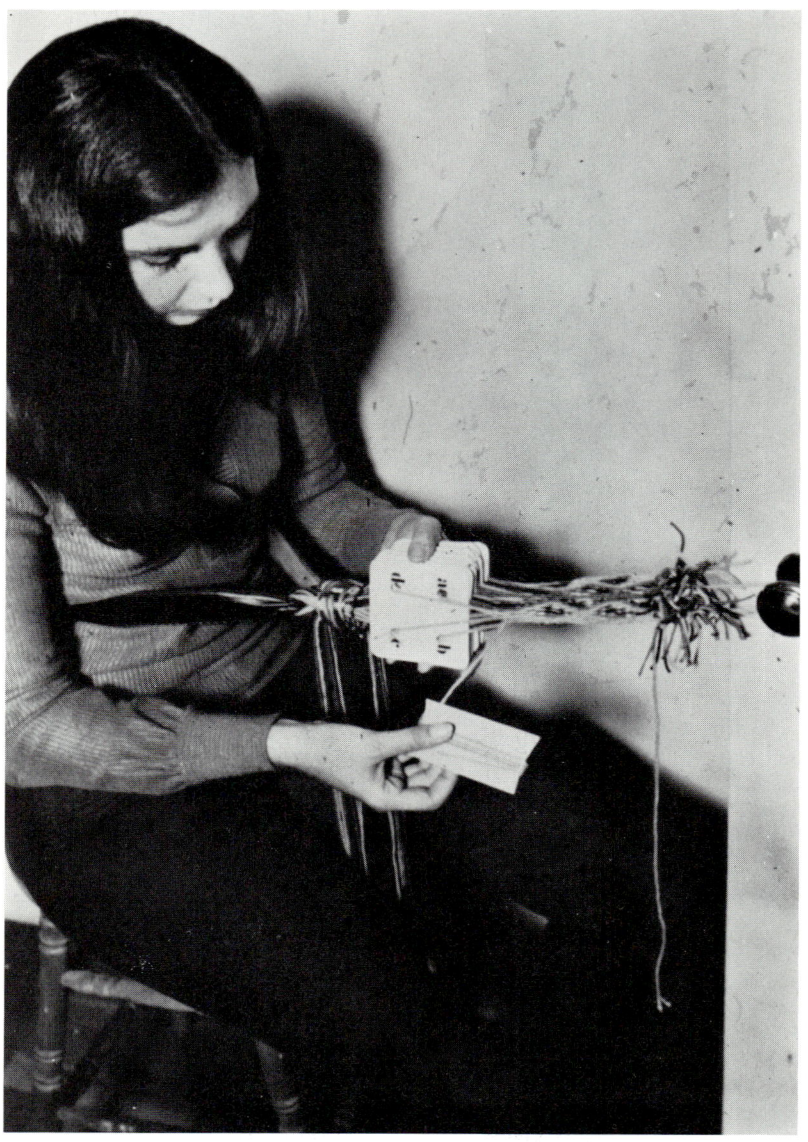

In card weaving, a pack of four-holed threaded cards takes the place of a wooden frame loom. (Photo, S. Rawlings)

CHAPTER 1

CARD WEAVING AN INTRODUCTION

Card or "tablet" weaving, an ancient art which uses a set of four-holed cards instead of a frame loom and is believed to date back to the Bronze Age, is fast gaining popularity as a means of creative self-expression among today's artisans, amateurs and professionals alike. While the process itself is easy to grasp (a beginner can make a handsome belt or guitar strap in only a couple of hours), the patterns and shapes possible to achieve with the technique can be as simple or complex as the weaver's imagination directs. And basically the only equipment needed is some thread and an inexpensive set of cards, easily made at home out of heavy cardboard or bought commercially.

As in conventional frame loom weaving, card weaving creates a fabric by interlacing warp (lengthwise threads) and weft (cross threads). The warp threads in card weaving, however, are not stretched and fastened to a wooden loom as they are in frame loom weaving. Instead, one warp end is secured around the weaver's waist; the other around a convenient stationary object such as a doorknob. In this way, the weaver himself creates the tension of the warp by pulling back on his end of the warp threads. The cards hold and separate the warp threads —a function of the heddle and harness in frame loom weaving. So, together, the weaver, stationary end, and threaded cards take the place of the loom.

The actual weaving process involves turning the pack of cards either clockwise or counterclockwise and, after each turn, inserting the weft through the opening in the warp called the shed. This turning of the cards causes the four warp threads which pass through each card to twist together into one four-ply strand. When the weft is passed through the shed, it draws the four-ply strands together and locks them into place. It is this twisting of the warp threads which is unique to card weaving and which results in a characteristically strong fabric. Also characteristic of card woven fabric is the fact that it is warp-faced, which means that only the lengthwise or warp threads are visible in the finished material. Additionally, card weaving produces a typically narrow band of fabric because it is difficult for the weaver to hold more than a limited number of cards while weaving. Some contemporary weavers, however, are experimenting with ways to create much wider, less traditionally sized and shaped woven bands (see Chapter 6, Special Techniques).

The early Egyptians used card weaving and some students of the craft credit them with its invention, which explains occasional references to the technique as Egyptian card weaving. The practice, however, was not confined to Egypt alone, nor even to the Middle East as a whole. Substantial evidence shows that this particular form of weaving enjoyed widespread use throughout Europe and Asia as well.

In the early card weaving societies, the cards were made from a variety of materials including horn, bone, wood, and leather. The type of thread fabric used ranged from heavy, coarse materials such as jute, which made exceptionally strong bands good for animal halters, to highly decorative silks for trim or belts.

Today the imaginative card weaver uses a wide assortment of materials and combinations of materials to create everything from sculptural wall hangings to sturdy luggage racks to contemporary vests and shoulder bags. Whatever the creation, whether purely aesthetic or strictly practical, the card weaver necessarily deals with four design elements: pattern, color, texture, and size. It is the particular combination of these elements decided upon by the weaver which gives the finished piece its creative individuality. The combinations possible are endless.

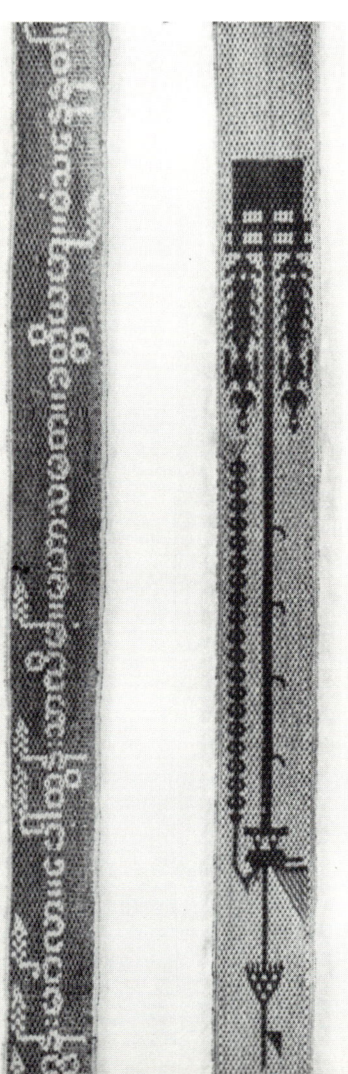

Card woven tape from Burma used to tie palm leaf manuscripts. The inscription is in Pali. (Courtesy of the Cooper-Hewitt Museum of Decorative Arts and Design, Smithsonian Institution)

16th-century ecclesiastical stole from Cologne, Germany. Silk, linen, and metal. (Courtesy of the Cooper-Hewitt Museum of Decorative Arts and Design, Smithsonian Institution)

"Totem." Joan Sterrenburg. Card woven strips made from natural dyed jute and silk were interlaced and plaited to make this 3' x 6½' wall hanging. (Photo, courtesy of the artist)

Belt. Mary Anne Mauro. Wool. (Photo, Jim Mauro)

Luggage rack. Sally Specht. Five card woven bands were secured to a wooden frame to make this folding luggage rack.

Shoulder bag. Robert Cranford. 2-ply worsted yarn. (Photo, Bob Warner)

Shoulder bag. Robert Cranford. The bag is finished with a velveteen lining. (Photo, Bob Warner)

CHAPTER 2

TOOLS AND MATERIALS

All you need to begin card weaving is some thread, a set of four-holed weaving cards, scissors, a rubber band, an old belt big enough to fit around your waist with several inches to spare, and a small shuttle—either homemade out of cardboard or commercially produced. If you make your own cards, you will also need a 3/8" paper punch. This is larger than the standard paper punch but should be available at most office supply stores.

You can use practically any type of fiber as long as it has good tensile strength. The finer the fiber, however, the greater the intricacy and detail of pattern. Card weavers use smooth fibers such as rattail and rayon slide cord as well as rough fibers such as sisal and jute, both separately and in combination, to create finished pieces with varying textural effects. The technique is so versatile that some weavers even work with such unconventional weaving materials as fishline and electrical cord.

The tools needed for card weaving include a belt which fits loosely around your waist, a rubber band (the kind used for gathering your hair is the easiest to work with), a pack of four-holed weaving cards, one or two shuttles, and a pair of scissors. Here we show a set of commercially made weaving cards; the cardboard shuttles, however, are homemade.

Some smooth fibers suitable for card weaving are rattail, packaging cording, nylon cording, cotton cording, soutache, raffia, and rayon slide cord.

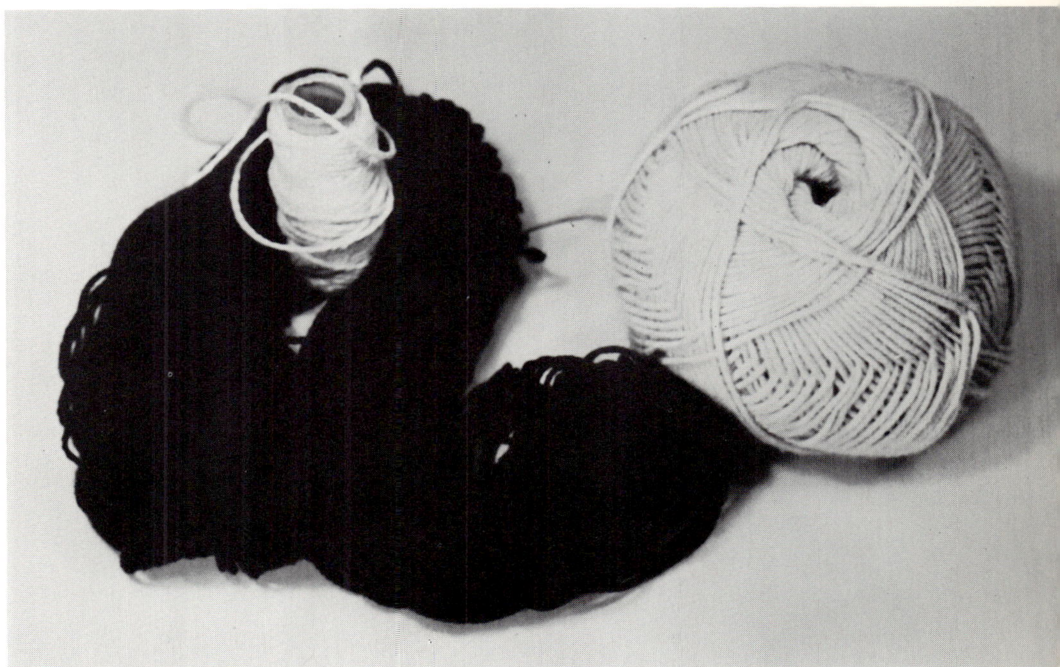

Some rough fibers used in card weaving are Persian rug yarn, jute, and orlon.

"Kawa." Kay Sekimachi. Nylon monofilament. Close-up of one small section of a 6' hanging. The nylon is so fine that the piece is only 1½" wide. (Photo, S. Rawlings)

"Aperture." Kathryn McCardle. A sculptural card-woven hanging of clear plastic, electrical cord, and tie-dyed silk. (Photo, courtesy of the artist)

Inexpensive ready-made cards can be purchased either directly or by mail order from a number of suppliers (see index for list of supply sources). Most commercially prepared cards are made from cardboard although some are plastic. Either type is good. Many weavers make their own cards out of heavy cardboard. Handy household sources of cardboard suitable for making the cards are numerous and include shoe boxes, the backs of writing tablets, and cardboard inserts in laundered shirts.

HOW TO MAKE YOUR OWN CARDS

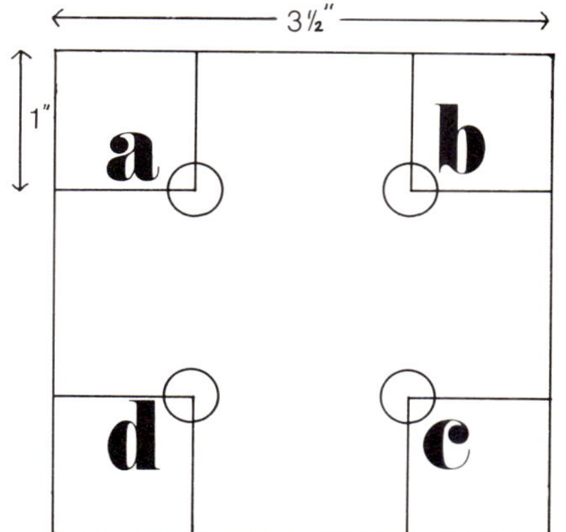

Draw a 3½" square on cardboard. (This size is easy to handle.) To determine the center of each of the four holes, make a 1" square in each corner of the card as shown. The point at which the two sides of each small square meet inside the big square marks the center of the hole. Using a ⅜" paper punch, punch out four holes. Letter each hole starting at the top left corner and continuing clockwise around the corners of the card.

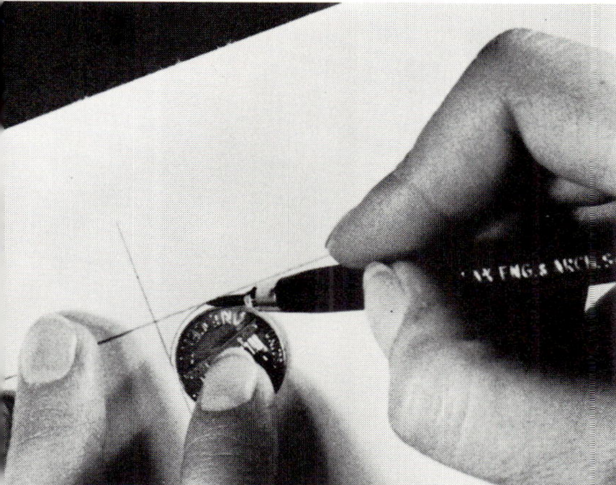

Use a penny as a guide for drawing rounded edges on the card. Cut along the guidelines. (Rounding off the edges makes the cards easier to work with in weaving.)

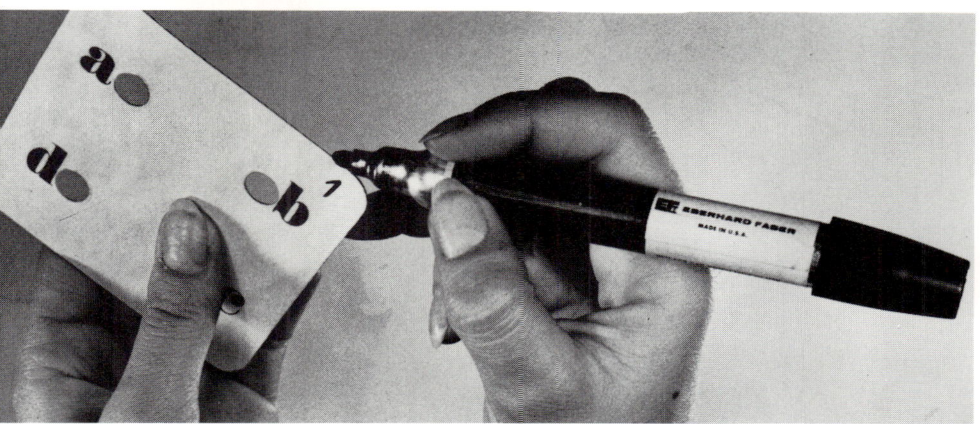

Mark the edge of each corner with a different color. Make the color markings the same for each card. (Felt tip pens or paints are good for this.) This will help you tell at a glance whether or not the cards are in the proper position while you are weaving.

CHAPTER 3

DRAFTING THE PATTERN

Before you start a project, it is a good idea to plan, on paper, the design you would like to weave. You do this by drafting a pattern, a relatively simple process which should help you avoid disappointing results.

1. First, determine what kind of thread you want to use and how wide a band you want to make. Once you do this, you can figure out the number of cards you should use for weaving the fabric. Each card adds to the width of the finished piece. The specific amount added depends upon the type and thickness of the fiber being used.

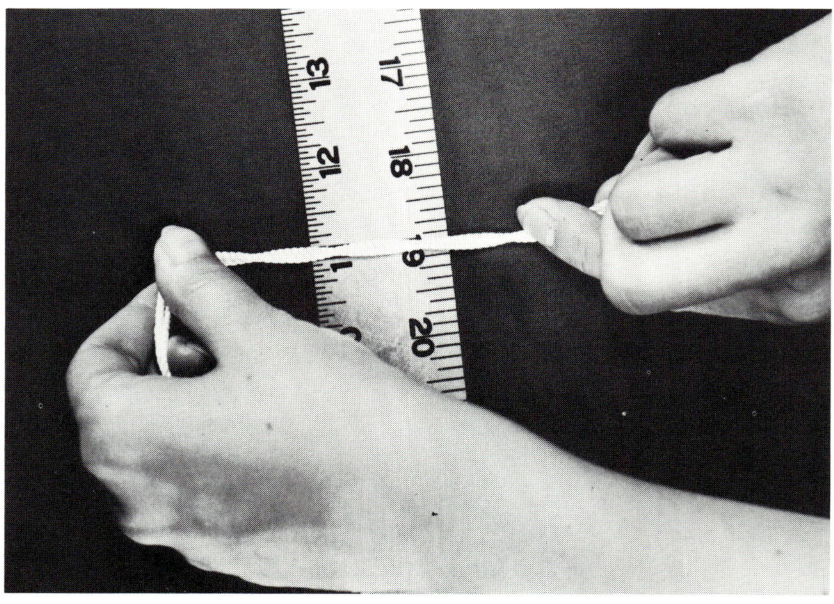

To estimate the amount added to the width of the fabric by a single card, twist together two of the thread fibers you will be using. The width of these two twisted cords equals the width added by each card.

2. Once you know how many cards you will be working with, use a piece of graph paper, if available, or square a plain sheet yourself to lay out the pattern.

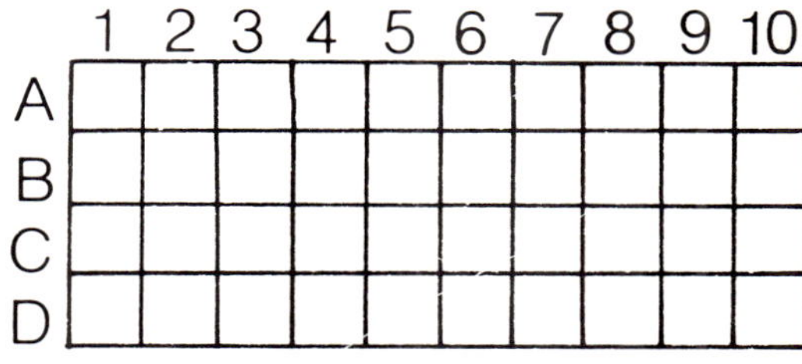

Mark off four squares down and letter each square A, B, C, and D. These letters correspond to the four holes in each card. Next, mark off one square across for each card you will be using. Here, we have marked off ten squares across showing that this pattern will be for a weaving which needs only ten cards.

3. Now, use two or more colors to fill in all the squares of your pattern block. (These colors represent the colors of your weaving threads). The way in which you arrange the colors of the squares determines the design. Later on when you prepare the cards, you will be using the graph as a threading color guide—each square of the graph represents a single threaded hole of the pack of cards.

   Below we show three examples of how you can achieve distinctly different designs with only two colors simply by rearranging the color placement.

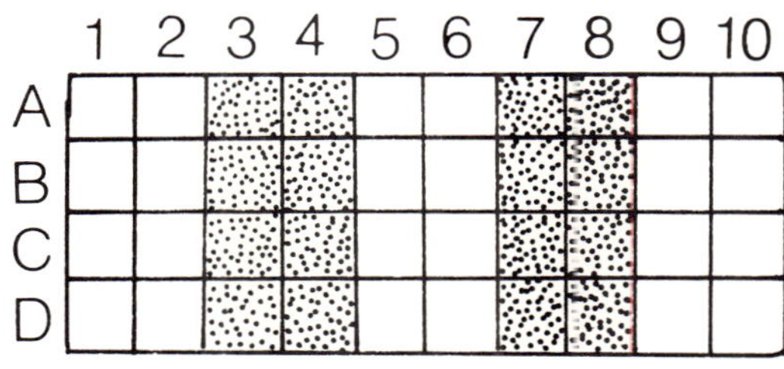

Striped pattern

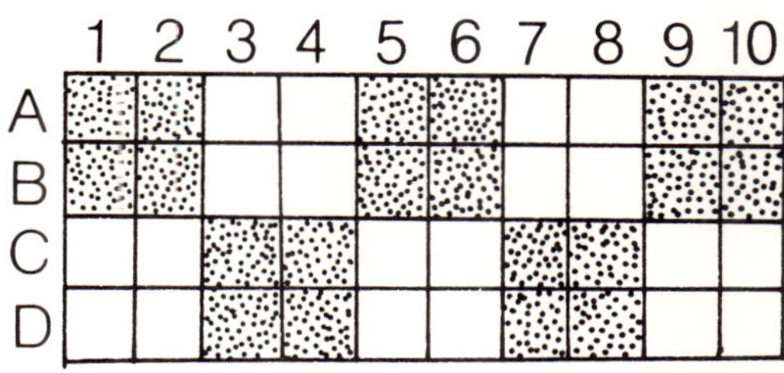

Checkerboard pattern

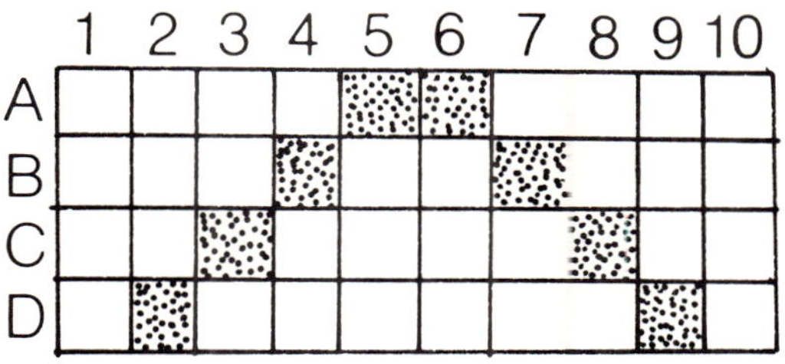

Chevron pattern

4. The direction of the turning cycle of the cards determines whether you repeat or reverse the drafted pattern block in your weaving. This should be a consideration in working up the total design effect you wish for the piece.

STARTING POSITION

The normal full cycle of counterclockwise *quarter turns.*

STARTING POSITION

The normal full cycle of clockwise *quarter turns.*

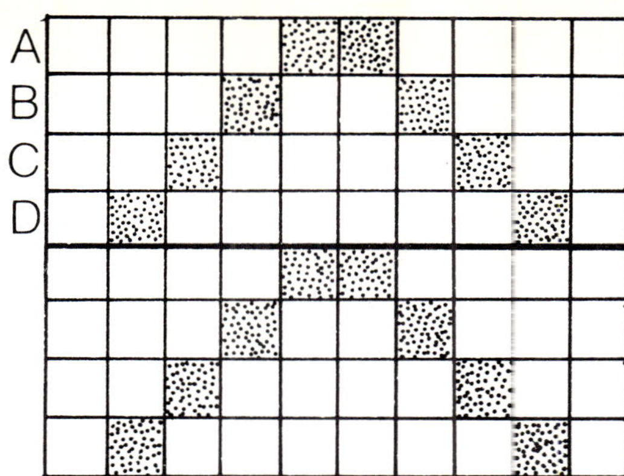

If the cards are turned counter-clockwise for two full cycles, the drafted pattern will be repeated.

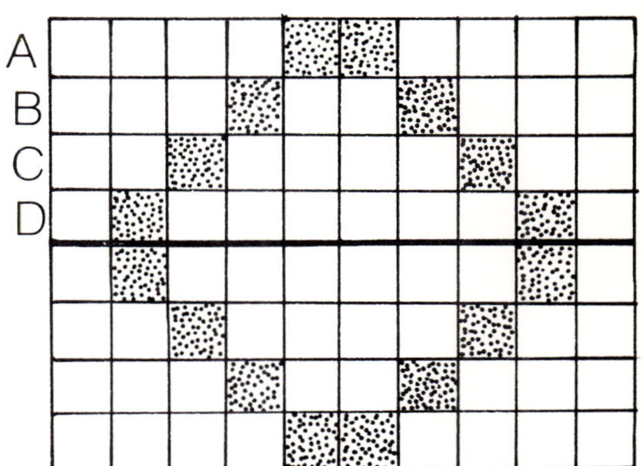

If one turning cycle is counter-clockwise and the next clockwise, the result will be the pattern and its mirror image.

5. It is a good idea to draw several pattern blocks and line them up one under the other in order to get a really good idea of how the finished strip will look. This is essential to do if you plan a carry-over design which requires repeating the pattern block two or more times.

1 2 3 4 5 6 7 8 9 10 11 12 13 14

Here the chevron actually needs three blocks to be seen in its entirety.

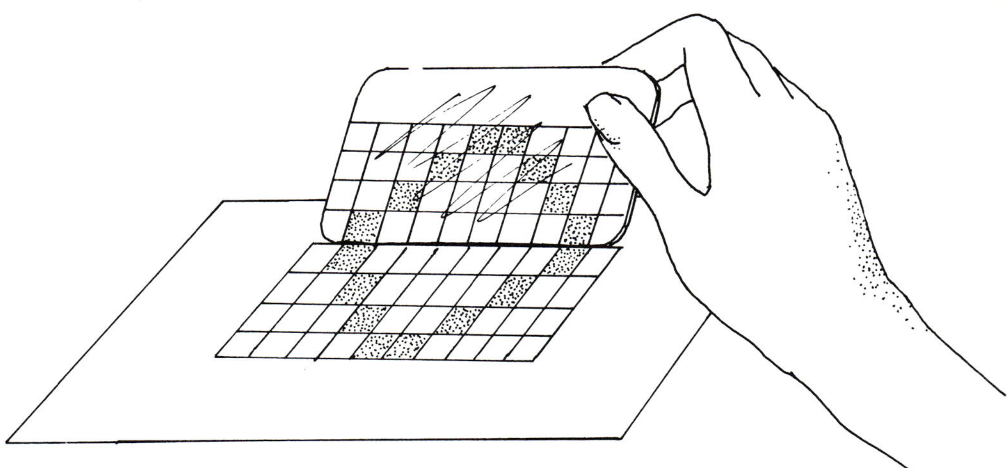

An easy and quick way to see what the pattern block and its mirror image will look like is to hold a small mirror up to the drafted pattern as shown. This will save having to draw out the mirror image on draft paper.

The reason you will be able to reproduce exactly what you draw up on graph paper is explained by what happens when you turn the pack of threaded cards during the actual weaving process. (A step-by-step explanation of the weaving process is presented in Chapter 5, Starting to Weave.)

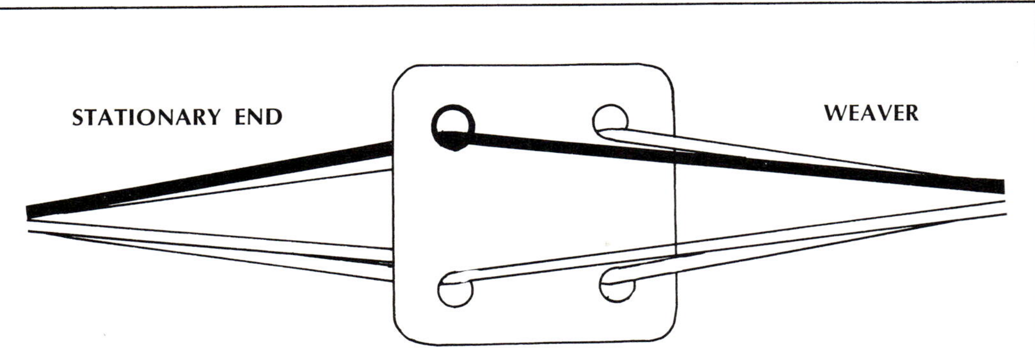

The hole in the upper left-hand corner of the cards is the "key" hole in card weaving. The thread which passes through it is the only one of the four which shows on the surface of the woven fabric. Before the cards are turned, this key hole thread of each card is always on top of the other three.

COUNTERCLOCKWISE

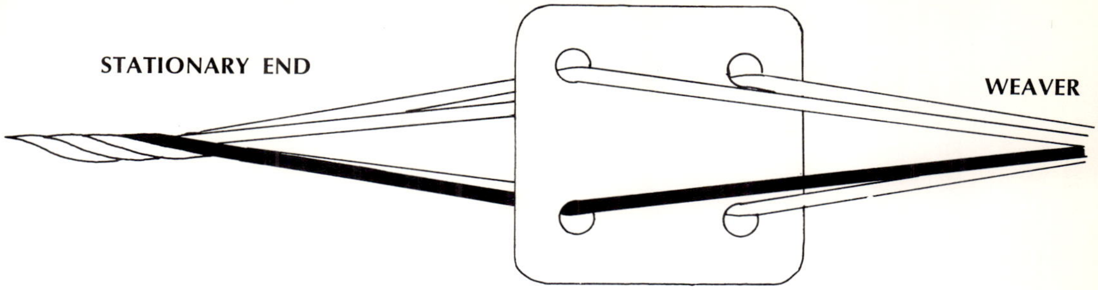

STATIONARY END

WEAVER

When the cards are turned a quarter turn counterclockwise the key hole thread moves down to the bottom of the pack and out of the key position. In the process, it twists around and therefore hides the other three threads. The twisted threads of all the cards are then locked into place by the weft and form a row of the fabric.

CLOCKWISE

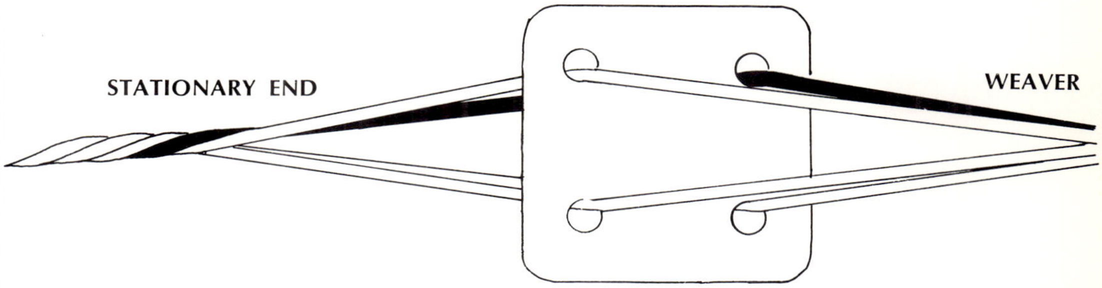

STATIONARY END

WEAVER

When the cards are turned a quarter turn clockwise, the key hole thread moves to the upper right-hand corner of the card and therefore out of the key position. In the process, it too twists around and hides the other three threads. The twisted threads of all the cards are then locked into place by the weft and form a row of the fabric. The only difference here from turning the cards counterclockwise is the direction in which the key thread twists around the other three threads.

So, if all the A hole threads of the pack of cards are in the upper left-hand position and you turn the pack a quarter turn, you will get a row of fabric which looks exactly like row A of the draft. Similarly, if the B hole threads are in the upper left position and you turn the pack a quarter turn, you will get a row of fabric which corresponds to row B of the draft, and so forth for holes C and D.

The one exception to the above occurs when the direction of the turns is changed. Note that the fourth quarter turn of either cycle will always bring up hole A into the key top left position. When the cards are turned in the reverse direction, however, these A hole threads do not twist around the others and do not show up in the fabric surface. This is true only at the point of reversal so the following key hole threads will form the visible part of the next row as usual.

CHAPTER 4

SETTING UP

The first step in setting up your cards and thread for weaving is to make the warp (lengthwise threads). A good rule of thumb is to cut each warp thread 1½ times the desired length of the finished woven band. This may be more than you need but it is difficult to estimate how much take-up there will be in the weaving process and it is always best to have more warp than necessary. If you want to leave extra warp for fringe on your weaving be sure to include the length of the fringe in the measurement of the finished band.

You will need to cut enough warp threads to equal four times the number of cards you are using. This will give you one thread for each of the four holes of every card you use.

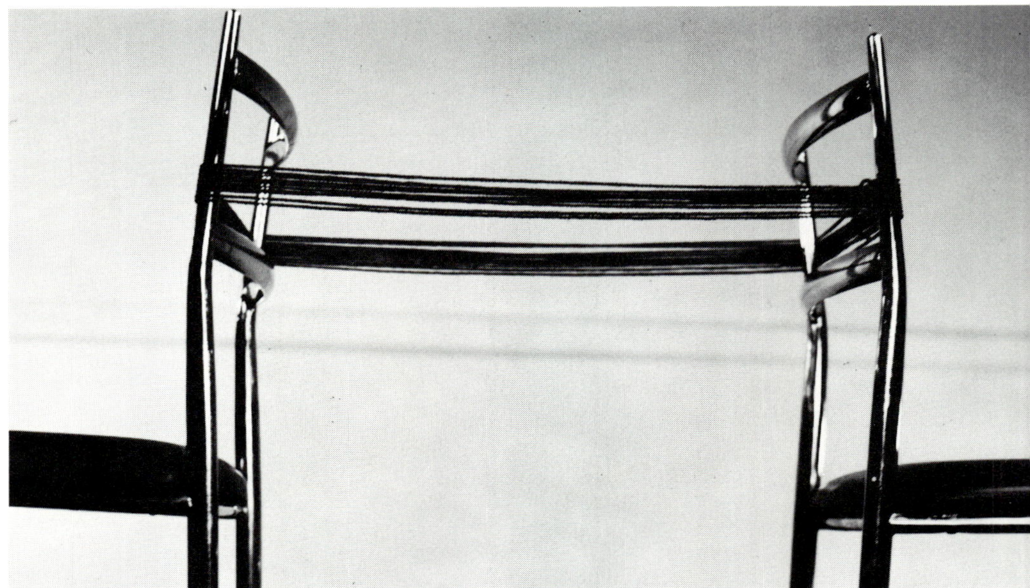

A good way to make the warp is to wrap the thread around two chairs (or other handy stationary objects) which are a distance apart equal to the desired length of the warp. After you have wrapped enough cord to make the required number of warp threads, cut both ends. This should save you a good deal of time.

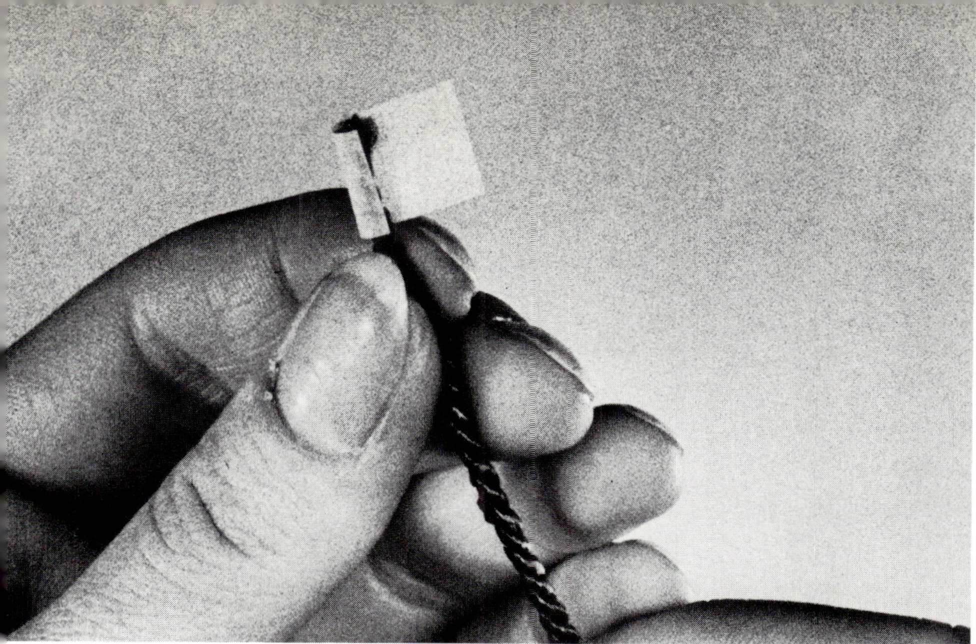

If you work with thread that tends to fray, it is a good idea to wrap masking tape around the ends of each warp thread you cut.

The next step is to thread the cards, using the drafted pattern as a guide. The colors used to thread the holes of each card should correspond to the colors charted out in the pattern. You can thread the cards either from the front of the card to the back or back to front.

Threading card front to back.

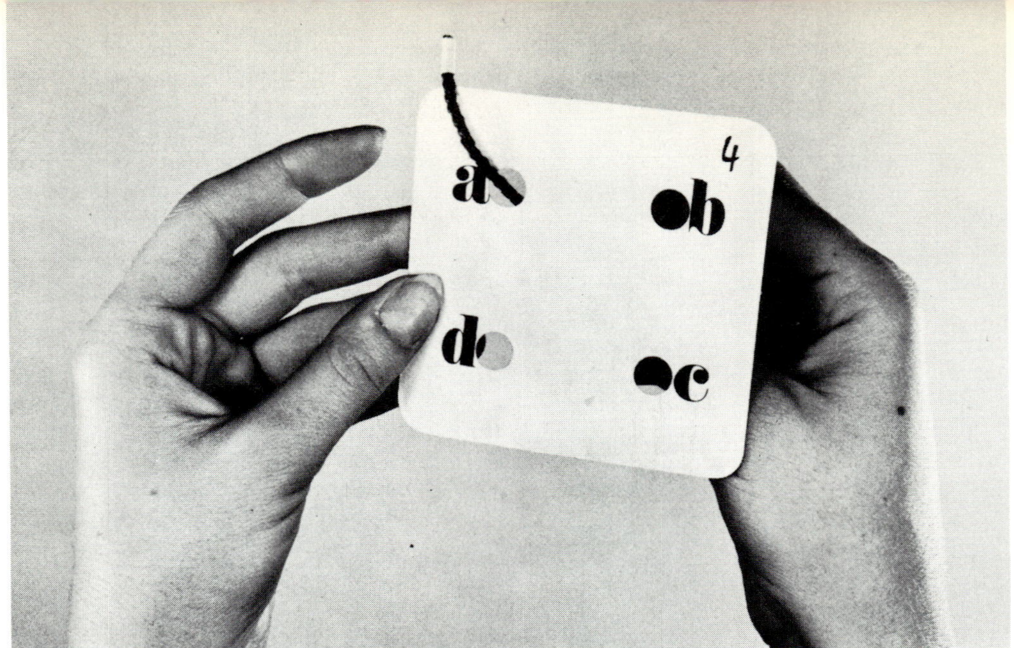

Threading card back to front.

As already noted, one of the unique characteristics of the card weaving technique is its twisting of the warp threads into four-ply strands during the actual weaving process. The result is a finished fabric made up of woven warp threads which, rather than being straight (i.e., plain weave) as they are in most types of weaving, are twisted or slanted to either the left or right.

The warp threads of this finished piece of card weaving have a left-hand twist on the left half of the weaving and a right-hand twist on the right half.

You will want to thread the cards so that the slant of the twist complements the drafted pattern.

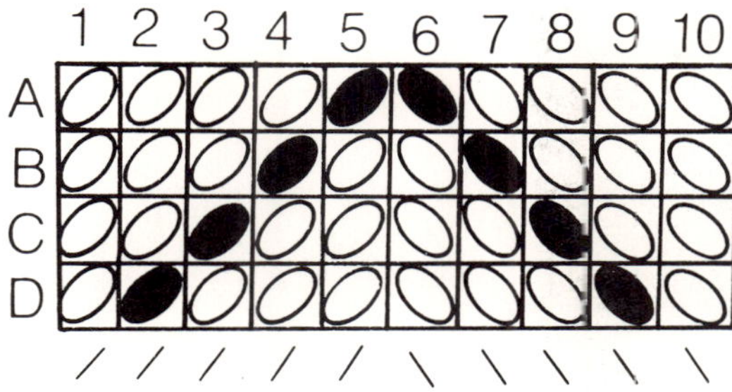

Cards 1-5 are threaded front to back; cards 6-10 back to front.

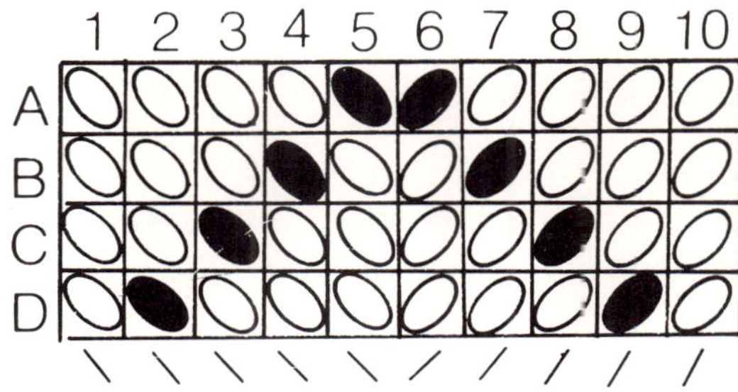

The opposite threading would produce a different twist effect. Cards 1-5 are threaded back to front; cards 6-10 front to back.

Note that although you can change the threading direction from card to card, you must thread the four holes of each card in the same way.

As you decide which way to thread your cards, you should indicate the direction on your drafted pattern for future reference. The standard way to do this is to place a slanted line or arrow underneath the numbered card columns of your draft. A downward line (\ ) means thread from back to front. An upward line (/) directs threading from front to back.

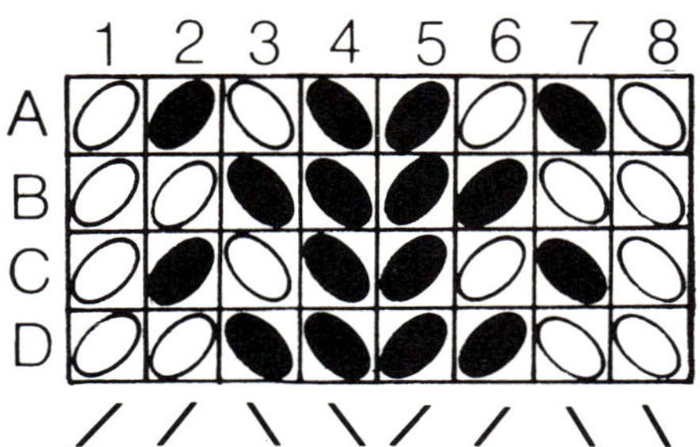

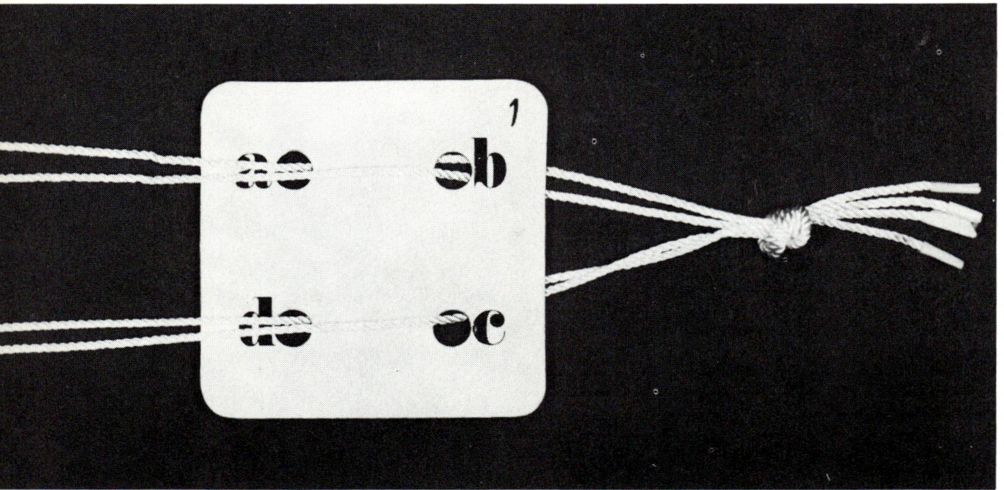

These four cards have been threaded in accordance with the first half of the pattern.

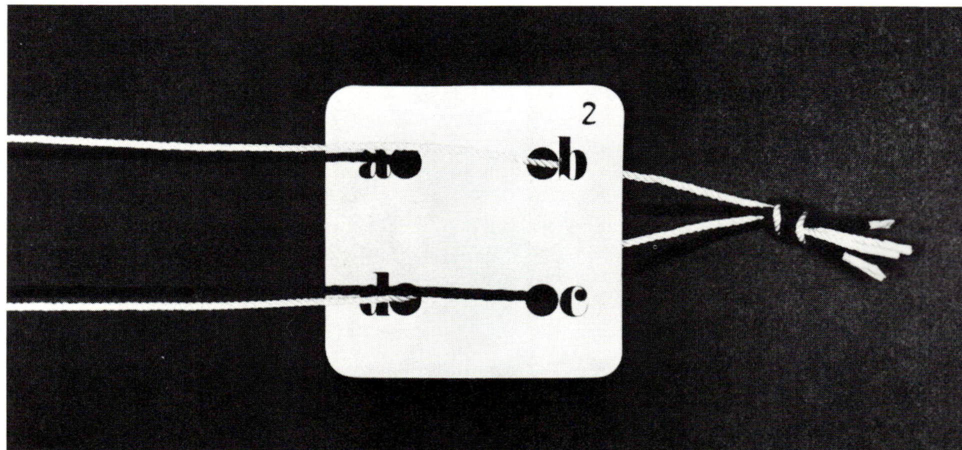

As you see, each of the holes (A, B, C, D) of the cards has been threaded correctly with either dark or light cord and cards #1 and #2 are threaded front to back; cards #3 and #4 back to front as directed.

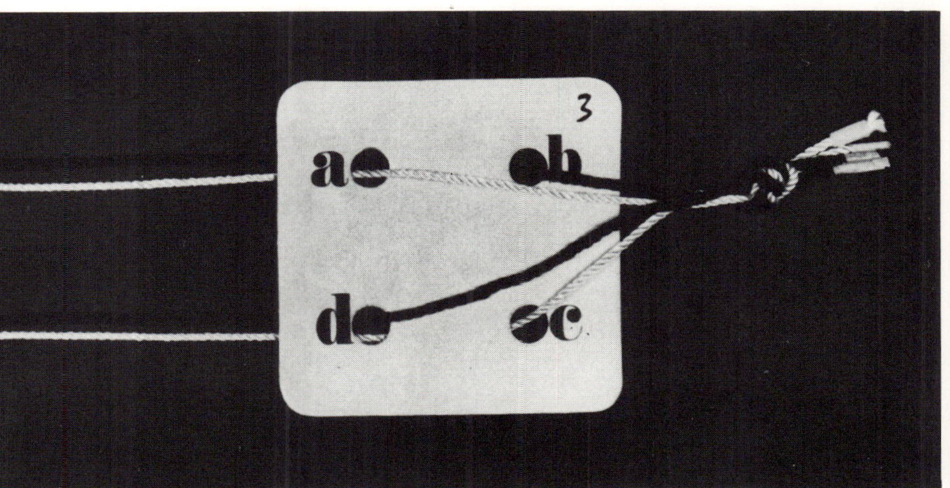
3
a
b
d
c

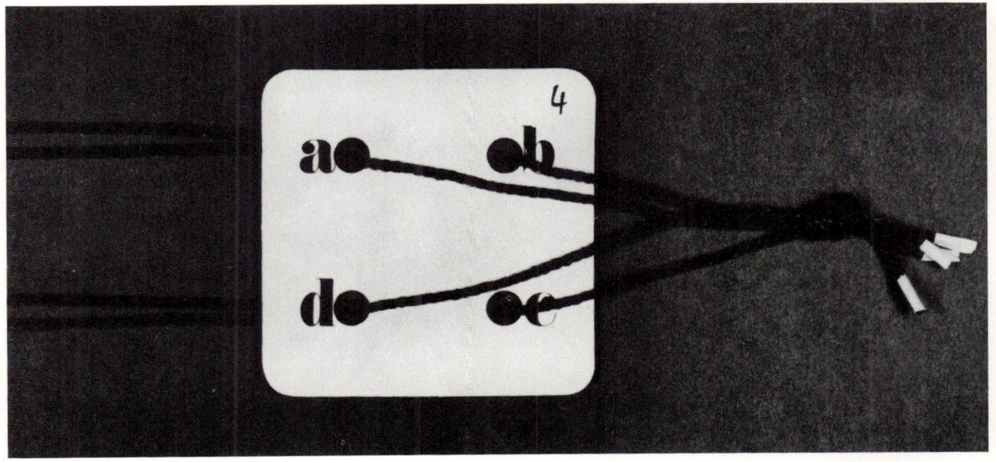
4
a
b
d
c

After you thread each card, knot the four thread ends together with an overhand knot.

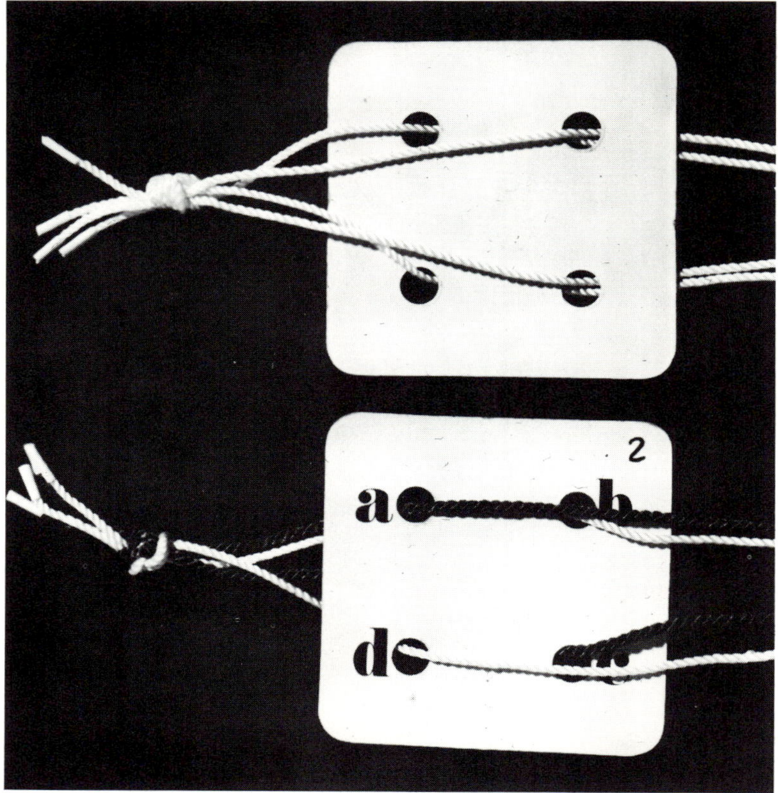

Thread and stack the cards in numerical order so that card #1 is on the bottom of the pack and the highest numbered card on the top. Be sure to stack the cards with the lettered side facing down, and with A and B at the top half and C and D at the bottom.

Once all the cards have been threaded and stacked, secure the pack with a rubber band. This will keep the cards in place and make the pack more manageable until you are ready to start weaving. Finally, run a piece of cord through the loops created by the knotted warp ends. Tie the ends of this cord together, again using the overhand knot.

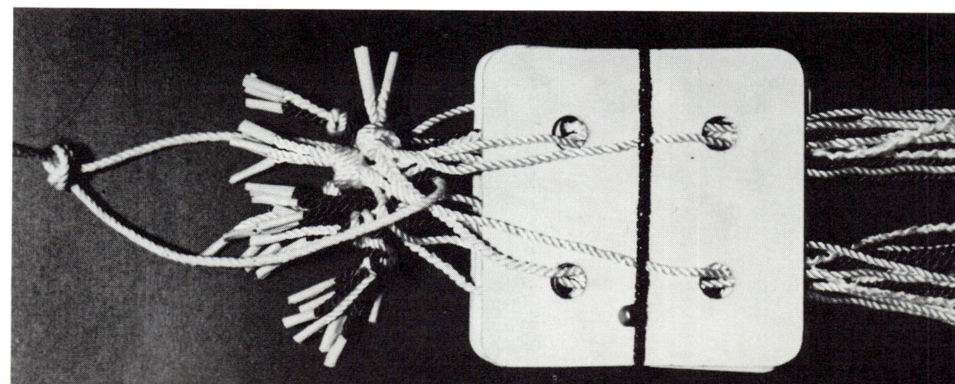

CHAPTER 5

STARTING TO WEAVE

Before you can start to weave, you will have to locate a stationary object to which you can secure the cord binding the knotted warp ends. Many household items are good for this purpose, including a sturdy chair arm or leg, a large hook projecting from the wall, or a doorknob as we show here. You can even move your setup outdoors and use a small tree trunk as your stationary end. You should also put on your belt before you start. Turn the buckle of the belt to the back.

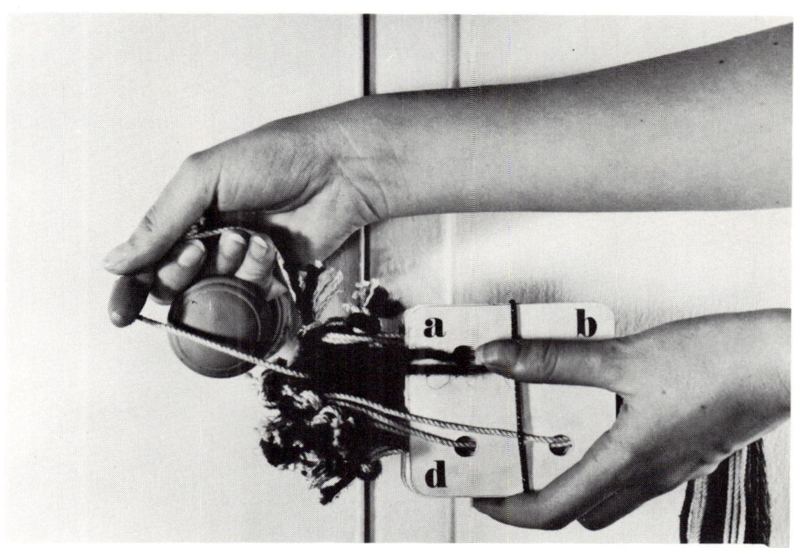

Loop the cord over a doorknob or whatever you decide to use as a stationary end.

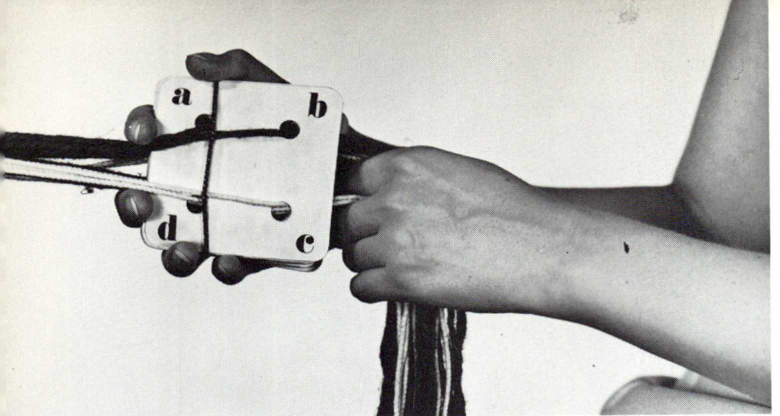

Next, create an even tension on all the threads by pulling the cards toward you. It is a good idea at this point to double-check that the A and B side of all the cards is showing on top as indicated.

Now you are ready to tie the loose thread ends around your belt with a special knot which is equally easy to tie and untie.

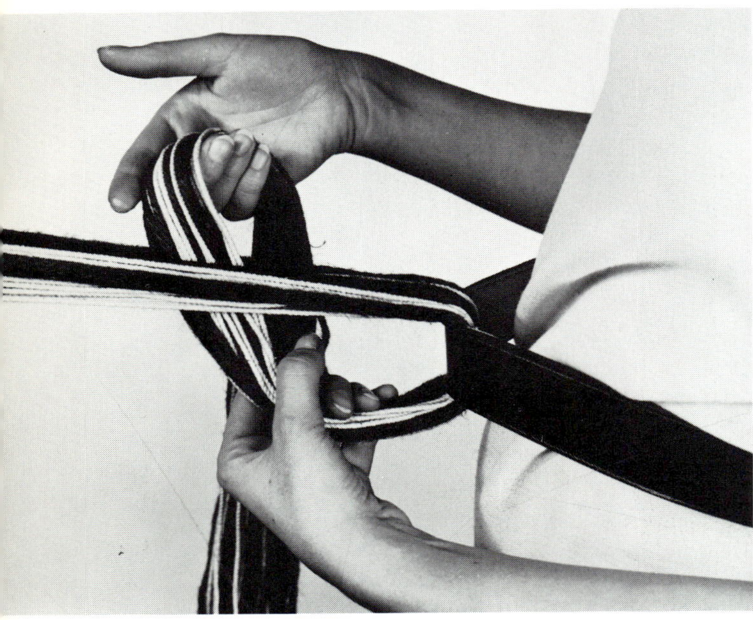

First, drop all the threads down over the belt as shown. Hold the threads together and taut with your left hand just below the belt. With your right hand, bring the slack ends up through approximately the middle of the taut part of the threads.

Once you have pulled the slack ends all the way through the middle opening, divide the threads roughly in half like this (each hand holds a half).

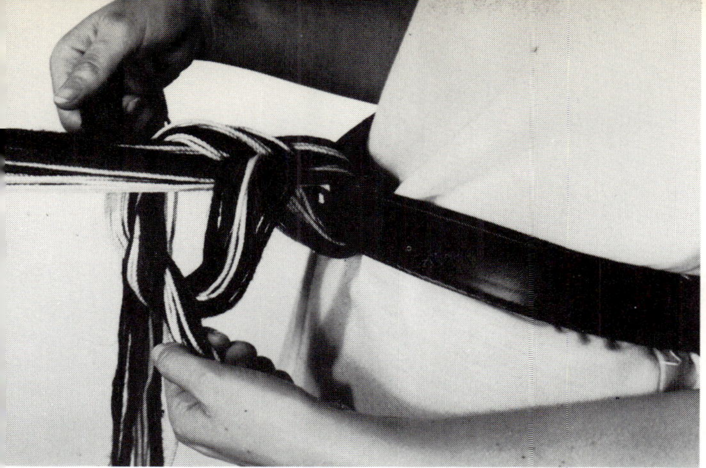

Use a bowknot to tie the two halves together underneath the taut threads. The knot is completed.

The lengthwise threads (warp) are now ready and you can begin to weave. Remember that you regulate the amount of tension on the warp threads with your back. The warp should be taut while weaving.

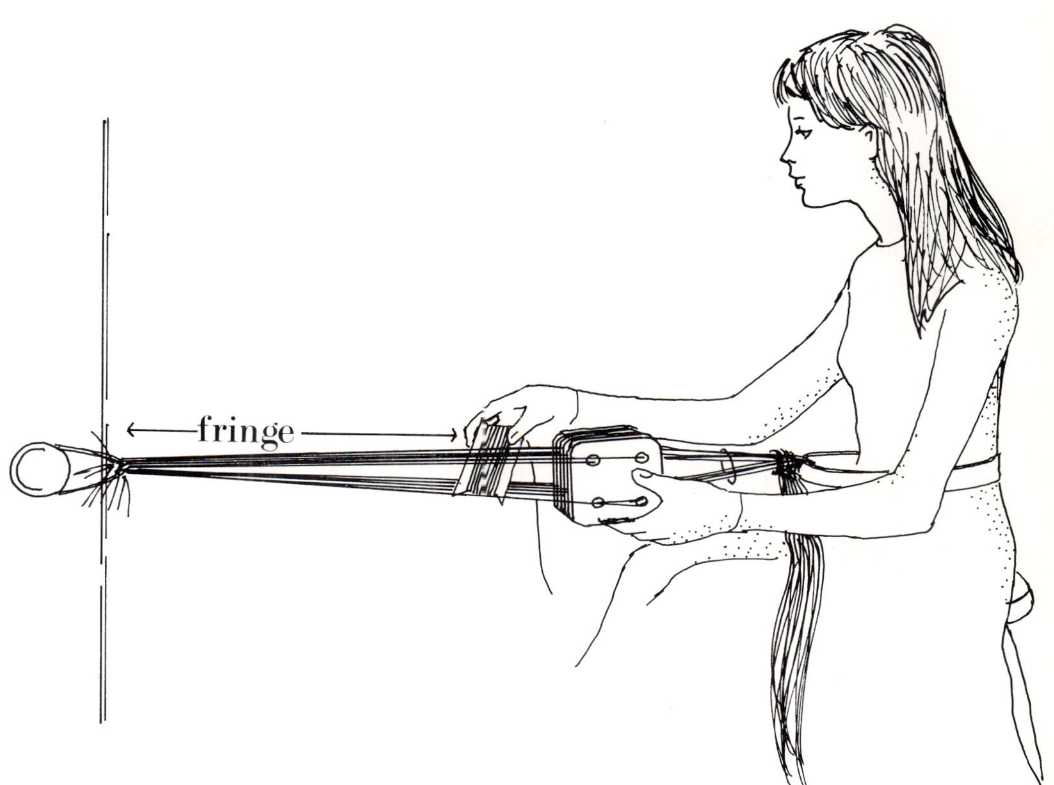

Start at the warp end opposite you and work toward yourself. If you want fringe, start the cross weave a distance from the knotted warp end equal to the desired length of the fringe. Note that you remove the rubber band from the cards toward you once you start weaving. (It is also possible to start at the end closest to your lap and work the weaving away from yourself. If you do this, however, you must coil the finished weaving as you progress in order to keep the pack of cards within reach. We find the other method works better.)

There are two ways of working the weft:

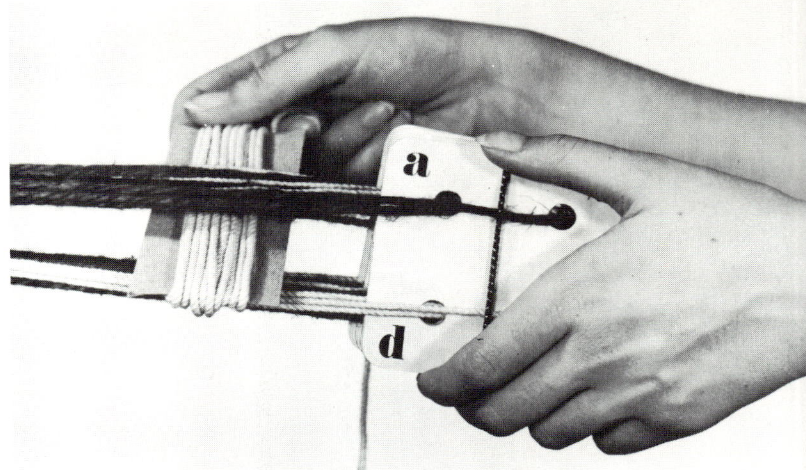

First, you can wind the weft around a cardboard shuttle and weave back and forth with only one end.

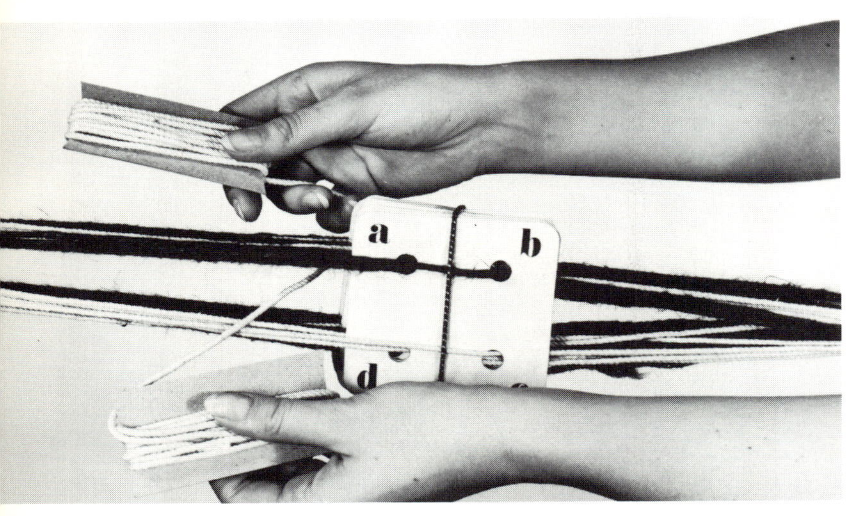

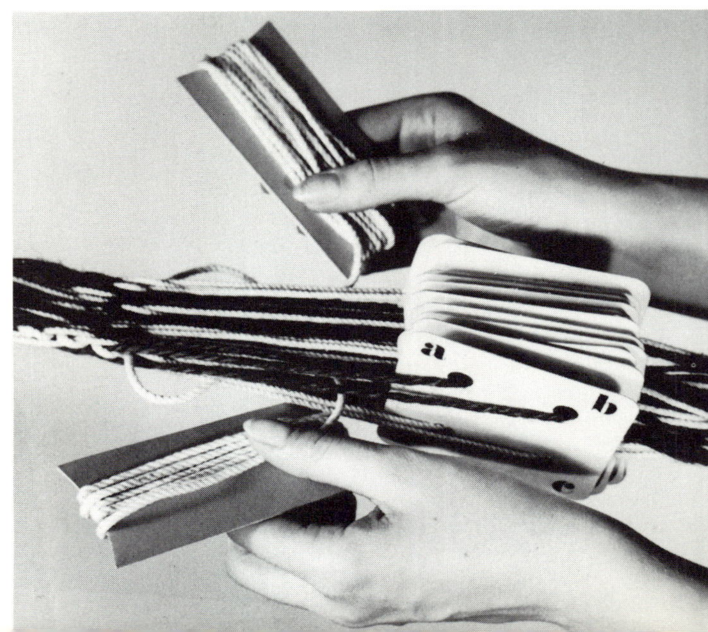

Or you can wind both ends of the weft thread around two shuttles and simultaneously weave both ends back and forth through the shed, working one weft end from right to left and the other from left to right. The two weft ends will cross each other and create a double thickness. The advantage of the double wefting method is that it locks in the weft, creating a more secure finished weave.

The double weft method is recommended for working with smooth, slippery thread fabrics such as rattail. If, on the other hand, you use one of the rougher materials such as jute or wool, which tend to hold in place on their own, the single weft method will do the job very well.

Whichever way you choose, try to wind enough thread to complete the project. It is simplest just to try to make a good estimate of how much weft you will need to complete the band. If you do run out before finishing, you can weave in new weft. Should this happen, weave in the new weft along with the tail end of the original weft for four or five turns of the cards. This should secure the new weft.

After passing the weft through the shed, turn the cards a quarter turn either clockwise or counterclockwise, depending upon the pattern which you are following. Then insert the weft once again.

If you choose to turn your cards all the same way throughout your weaving, you will find the warp threads will become twisted. When this happens, release the warp threads from your belt, untwist the threads (it is easier if you do it card by card) and retie them to your belt. If, on the other hand, you alternate the turning cycles, the warp threads will not twist since, by reversing the direction in which you turn your cards, you will be undoing any twists you have created.

Turning the cards in the same direction causes the finished band to have a tendency to spiral while hanging free. Some weavers use this to their advantage.

"Shaman's Shrine Piece." Joan Sterrenburg. 3′ x 4′. Wool, horsehair, cowhair. In this piece the artist takes advantage of the tendency of card woven bands to spiral if woven by turning the cards in the same direction. (Photo, courtesy of the artist)

"Shaman's Shrine Piece." Joan Sterrenburg. Detail. (Photo, courtesy of the artist)

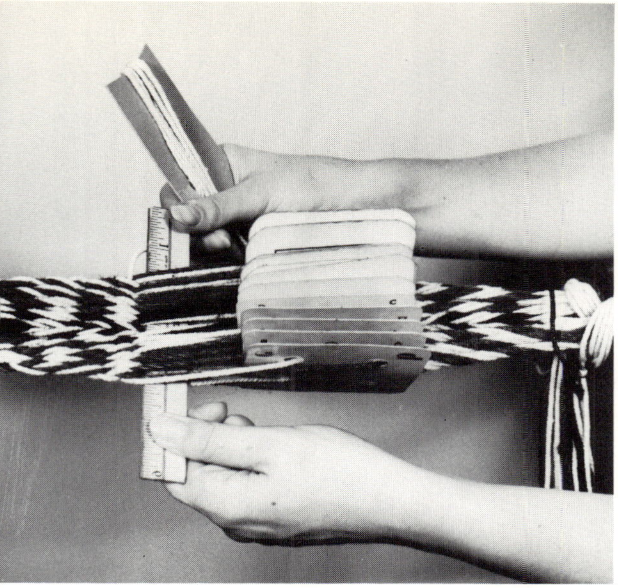

After each turn, use a ruler or some other flat sturdy object (a wooden shuttle works well) to push the previous weft thread back toward the knotted warp ends. This will ensure against a flimsy, irregularly finished piece. Then pass the new weft through the shed. (Photo, S. Rawlings)

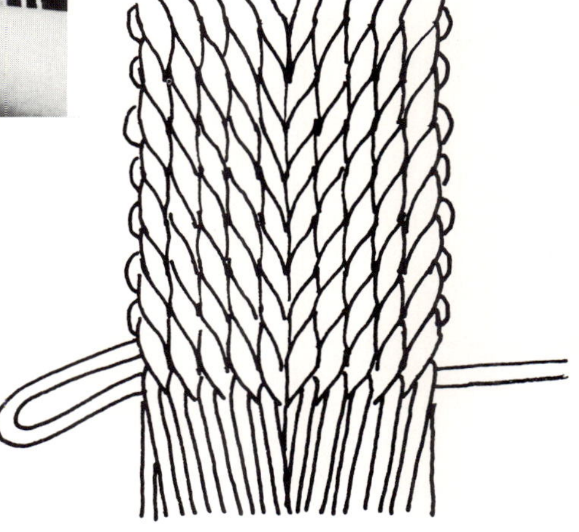

When you insert the weft through the shed, leave a loop of slack weft on the side as illustrated. Turn the cards a quarter turn, beat the threads back, and then pull the weft tight. Repeat this process throughout the weaving. This helps to make the edges of the woven piece even.

Continue this entire weaving process until you have woven the band to the desired length.

There are several ways to finish the band. The one to use depends upon the wefting method.

To end a single wefted band, just remove the cards and let the unwoven weft thread hang loosely with the unwoven warp threads to form a fringe.

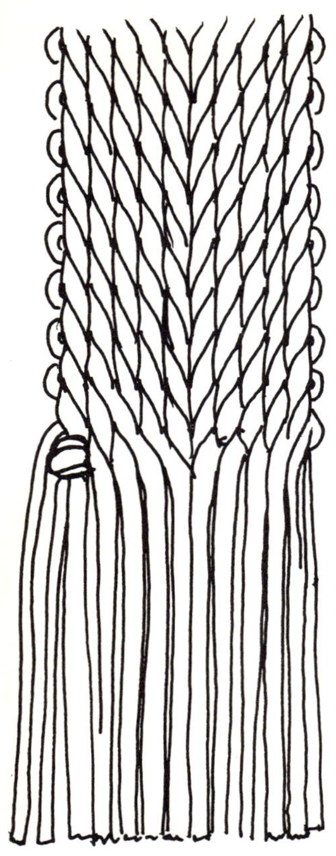

Or, let the weft thread hang loosely but tie a knot in several of the warp threads that form the fringe.

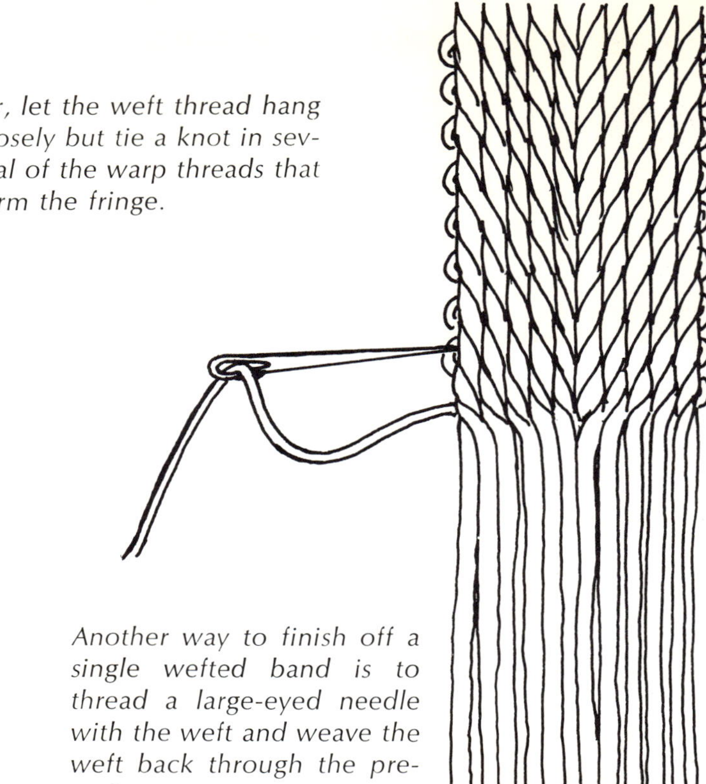

Another way to finish off a single wefted band is to thread a large-eyed needle with the weft and weave the weft back through the preceding row.

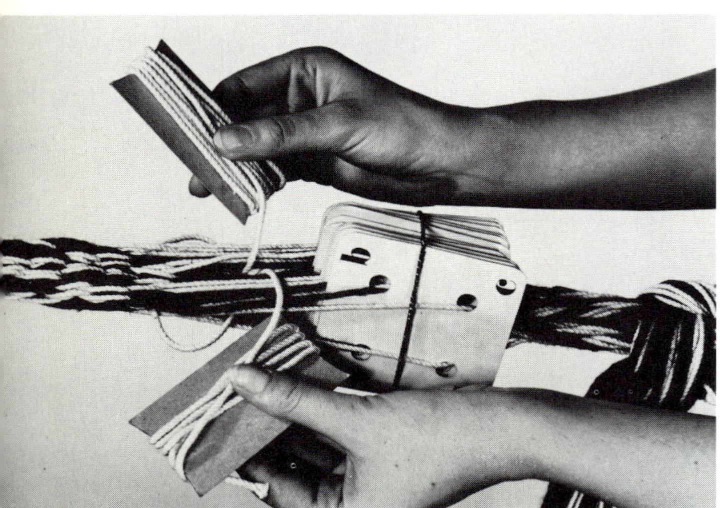

To finish the double wefted band, bring the two weft ends up through approximately the middle of the taut, unwoven warp threads.

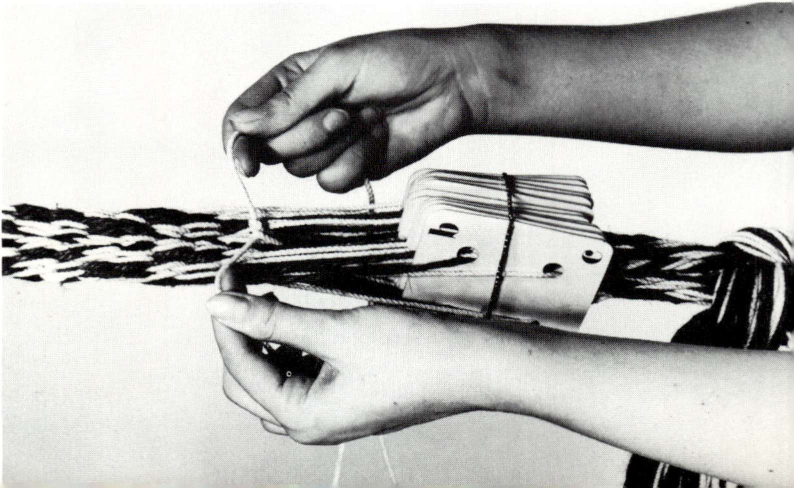

Now tie the ends together with a square knot. Remove the cards.

Placemat. Sally Specht. Spinnerin Polypropylene twine. Photo, Sandra Rawlings

Shoulder bag. Robert Cranford. Photo, Bob Warner

"Inner Space." Lillian Elliott. 15" × 30". Wool. Card weaving with embroidery. Photo, Stone & Steccati, San Francisco

Belts on Fence. Sally Specht. Slide cord, rattail, cotton cording, ribbon, hat straw. Photo, Sandra Rawlings

Wall Hanging. Susan Lehman. Chenille, cotton, wool, linen, rayon bouclé, rayon. Photo, Sandra Rawlings

Bands. Robert Cranford. 2-ply Persian crewel yarn. Photo, Bob Warner

"Shaman's Shrine Piece." Joan Sterrenburg. 3′ × 4′. Wool, horsehair, cowhair. Card weaving, interlacing. Photo, courtesy of the artist

Vest Front. Sally Specht. Persian rug yarn. Photo, Sing-Si Schwartz

Vest Back. Sally Specht. Persian rug yarn. Photo, Sing-Si Schwartz

Ski or hiking boot laces. Sally Specht. Mercerized cotton.
Photo, Sandra Rawlings

Belt. Sally Specht. Rayon slide cord, hat straw. Photo, Sandra Rawlings

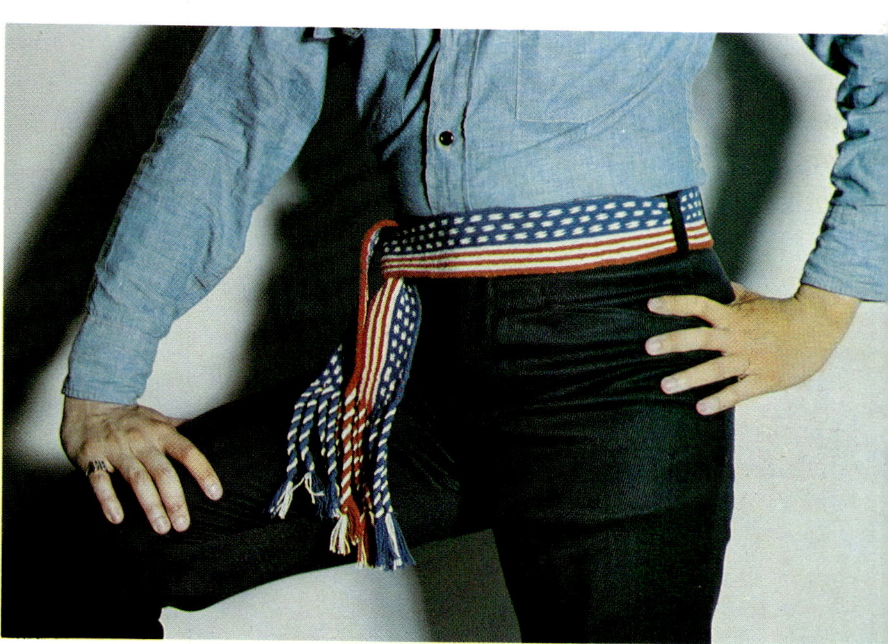

Flag Belt. Walter Seifert. Wool, nylon.
Photo, Sandra Rawlings

Planter. Sally Specht. Spinnerin Polypropylene twine.
Photo, Sandra Rawlings

Coasters. Sally Specht. Spinnerin Polypropylene twine.
Photo, Sandra Rawlings

Plant Mat. Maria Elena Arejula. Polished cable cord, cotton string. Photo, Sandra Rawlings

"Gregg's Hair." Phoebe McAfee. 12" × 48". Swedish wool.
Photo, Sol Columbus

"Indian." Phoebe McAfee. 12" × 50". Wool.
Photo, Sol Columbus

"Ode to Spring." Kathryn McCardle. Wool, jute, silk-screened linen. Photo, courtesy of the artist

"Totem." Joan Sterrenburg. 3′ × 6½′. Jute, silk. Card weaving, interlacing, plaiting. Photo, courtesy of the artist

"Horsehair Hanging." Lillian Elliott. 14″ × 36″. Wool, linen, horsehair, cotalin. Card weaving with binding. Photo, Stone & Steccati, San Francisco

"Tribal Cloth." Lillian Elliott. 6′ × 10′. Wool, mohair, fleece. Ikat and tie-dye. Photo, Stone & Steccati, San Francisco

Tent. Dorothy Field. Wool, sisal. Photo, Rudy vander Vegt

Blanket with Card Weaving Inserts. Lillian Elliott. 5′ × 7′. Wool. Photo, Gordon Holler

Shoulder bag. Jean Singerman. Ikat wool. Photo courtesy of the artist

CHAPTER 6

SPECIAL TECHNIQUES

You can change the overall design of your weavings dramatically by using a number of special card weaving techniques. Most of these techniques are simple enough for the beginner to try out immediately; some, however, are more complicated and probably will appeal to the more advanced weaver.

The significance of the many special techniques is, of course, the great latitude they afford the weaver. Not only can the pattern within the woven fabric be varied but also the very structure of the fabric itself can be changed. So endless, in fact, are the pattern possibilities in card weaving that some weavers limit themselves to experimenting only with pattern variation, using very fine multicolored threads and creating traditionally narrow, flat bands. Others emphasize the textural and structural possibilities. Whichever the emphasis, if any, the important point to note is that these possibilities do exist and that, as a consequence, the card weaving process can be individualized according to the approach and interest of each weaver. This is what makes card weaving exciting to a wide assortment of craftsmen and artists.

Bands. Robert Cranford. 2-ply Persian crewel yarn. (Photo, Bob Warner)

Untitled hanging. Barbara Shawcroft. 7′ x 20″. Horsehair, silk, alpaca. Card weaving, wrapping, and soumak. This is a section of a larger weaving, in process. (Photo, Lance Hughston)

"Horsehair Hanging." Lillian Elliott. 14″ x 36″. Wool, linen, horsehair, cotalin. Card weaving with binding. (Photo, Stone & Steccati, San Francisco)

1. CHANGING THE STARTING POSITION OF THE CARDS

If you maintain a 4-4 turning cycle for your cards (i.e., four quarter turns one direction; four reverse—see Chapter 3), you can alter the pattern of your band by starting the cards in any position other than with the A-B side on top as previously recommended. This way the pattern will start on the B, C, or D line of the paper draft.

These four patterns were made from the same threading but by using a different starting position of the cards for each one. (Photos, S. Rawlings)

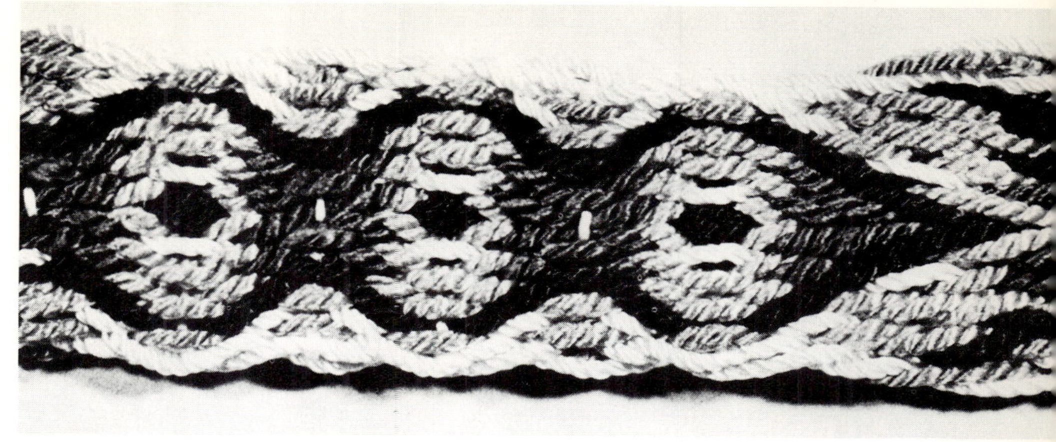

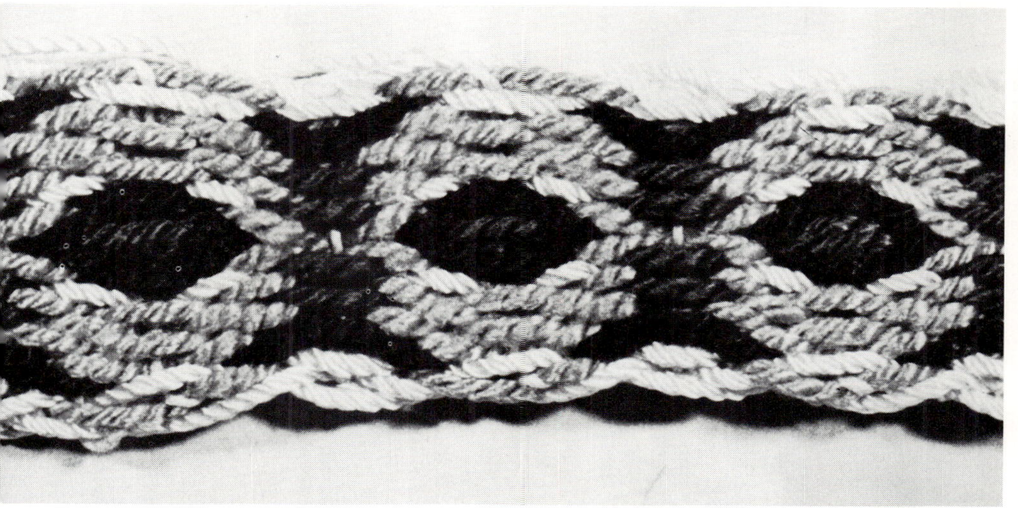

2. CHANGING THE TURNING CYCLE OF THE PACK OF CARDS

You can change the turning cycle from 4-4 or from all turns in the same direction to any number of turns clockwise or counterclockwise and in any combination. So, for instance, you could turn the pack 6 quarter turns in one direction, 4 in reverse, then 3 in the original direction, and so forth. The permutations are limitless. One turning combination of particular interest to note is the 2-2 turning cycle. By alternating the turning direction between two quarter turns one way and two reverse for the entire weaving, you will get a band in plain weave rather than the twisted warp-faced fabric typical of card weaving.

Changing the turning sequence of the cards creates multiple pattern effects.

The 2–2 turning cycle creates a plain weave. (Photo, S. Rawlings)

3. TURNING INDIVIDUAL CARDS

In addition to turning all the cards as a pack, you can turn each card independently. Although often complex, this kind of turning allows you to get not only multiple patterns from the same threading but also some of the most intricate patterns possible to achieve with card weaving. Below we describe two specific methods of working with this technique. While each gives the weaver considerable leeway in developing designs, neither represents a means of exploring the technique to the fullest. We suggest experimenting with your own ways of turning individual cards to vary the pattern as well as familiarizing yourself with the following.

Method 1

Turn one card (or more) a quarter turn in one direction and the rest of the pack a quarter turn in the opposite direction and insert the weft. Next, turn another card (or more) along with the first a quarter turn in the opposite direction from which you turn the pack. Again insert the weft. Continue this until you have reversed the turning direction of all the cards. Then repeat the process in the opposite direction.

The best results are achieved if the cards are threaded with only two colors, one for holes A and B and the other for holes C and D, and if you reverse individual cards systematically (e.g., reversing the cards one by one in numerical order; reversing every other card; reversing the middle card or cards and working out toward each side and so forth).

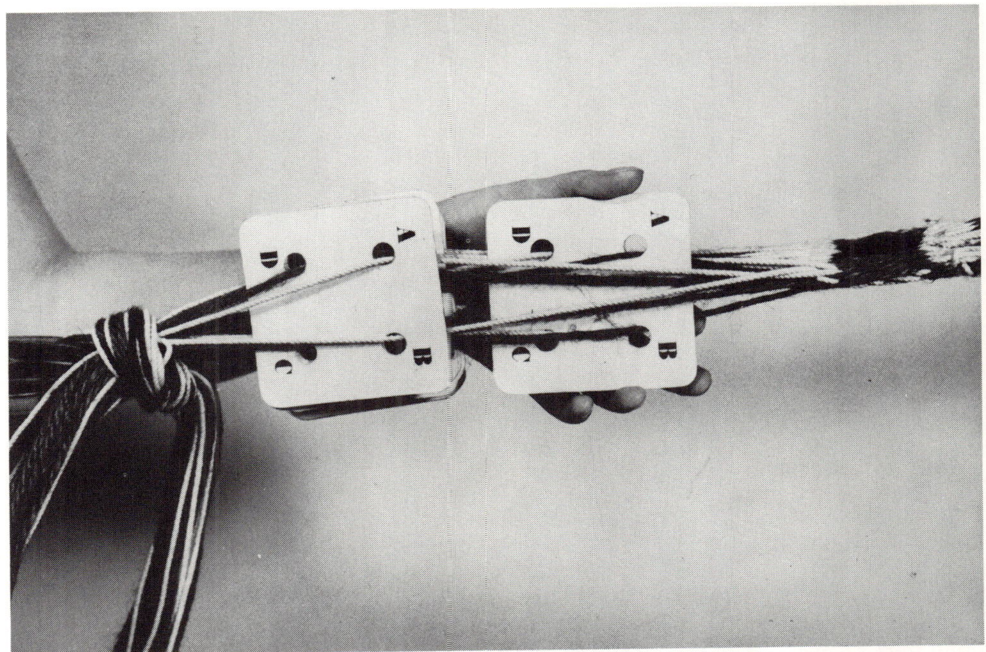

Whenever you are going to turn individual cards, it is easiest to slide them slightly forward on the warp, and then turn them. (Photo, S. Rawlings)

The elongated diagonals of this band were formed by systematically reversing individual cards.
Starting at the weaver's far right, two cards were turned a quarter turn in the opposite direction from the rest of the pack after each insertion of the weft until the turning direction of all the cards had been reversed. Then the process was repeated starting with the two outermost cards on the weaver's left.

Method 2

This method is most commonly used to weave names or messages into the band. It requires that the cards be threaded with only two colors, one for holes A and B and the other for holes C and D, and that the turning direction of the pack be alternated between two quarter turns counterclockwise and two quarter turns clockwise. This combination of threading and turning produces a plain weave fabric (i.e., the warps are not twisted) which is one color on the top side and the second color on the under side.

In between turns of the pack, individual cards must be turned separately in order to weave a letter or pattern. Specifically, turn those cards with which you wish to create the pattern two quarter turns (in the same direction in which you have been turning the pack) without inserting the weft. This will make the top and bottom colors of those cards change places. When all the cards are once again turned together as a pack in the alternating manner, the cards which were independently turned will weave the opposite color of all the other cards. The number and position of the cards which are turned individually, then, determine the letter produced.

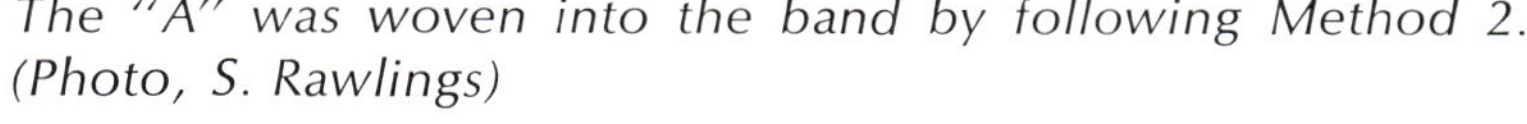

The "A" was woven into the band by following Method 2. (Photo, S. Rawlings)

"Gregg's Hair." Phoebe McAfee. 12" x 48". Swedish wool. The cards for this piece were divided into 5 groups and each group was threaded with only two colors—one color for the top two holes of each card and the second color for the bottom two holes. The pattern was formed by turning individual cards independently (Method 2) and by moving the cards sideways (see Chapter 6, Special Technique #9). (Photo, Sol Columbus)

4. TURNING WITHOUT INSERTING THE WEFT

By turning the cards several times in the same direction (either clockwise or counterclockwise) without inserting the weft after each turn, you can create an unwoven area containing only twisted warp threads. This "open space effect" can be effective in altering the total design of your weaving both aesthetically and functionally.

Here a piece of wood has been inserted in the unwoven, open space area created by turning the cards without inserting the weft.

5. WEAVING WITH THE CARDS IN A DIAMOND POSITION

If you change the normal weaving position of the cards to a diamond position, you will create two sheds in your warp. Card weaving with two sheds instead of one makes it possible for you to make four distinctly different types of fabric: double strip, connected double strip, tubular, and double cloth.

The key to most double shed weaving is the way in which you manipulate the cards before inserting the weft.

Position 1

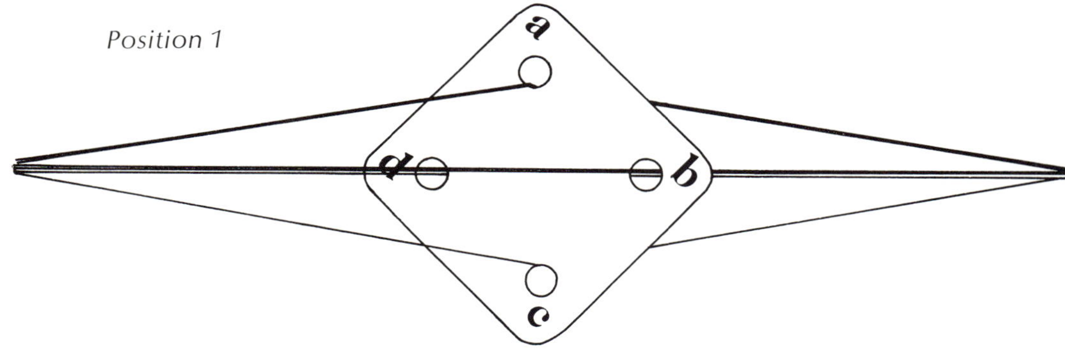

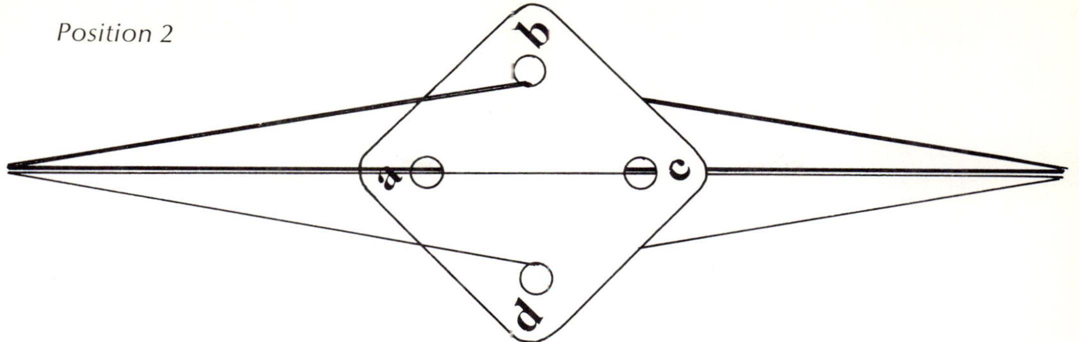

You actually rock the pack back and forth between positions 1 and 2 and insert the weft with each new position of the cards. This rocking of the cards keeps the upper and lower warp threads separate throughout the weaving.

a) *Double Strip*

If you use two wefts and insert one into each shed every time you rock the cards, you will simultaneously create two bands. Each of these finished bands will be in plain weave rather than the twisted warp weave of most card weaving.

Double strip. (Photo, S. Rawlings)

b) *Connected Double Strip*

By inserting the same weft through both sheds each time after you rock the cards, you can create two finished strips which are connected on one side—either the weaver's left or right side, depending upon the direction in which you insert the weft. You can use this technique in combination with regular card weaving to make a pocket.

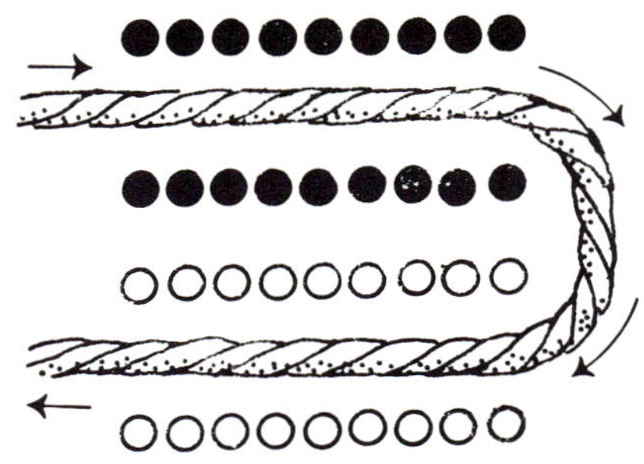
1.

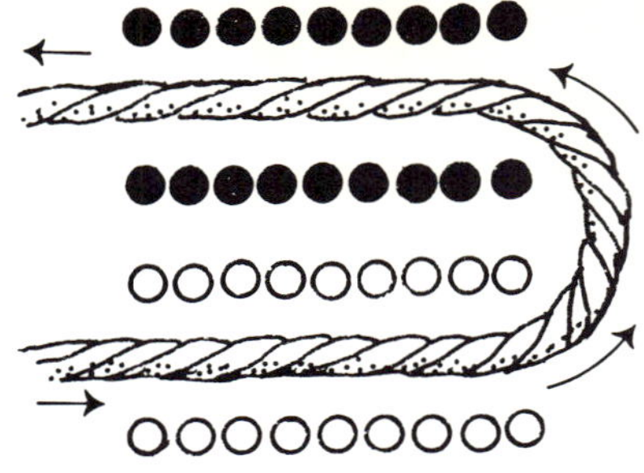
2. CONNECTED ON ONE SIDE

To connect the two strips on the weaver's right, insert the weft through the top shed from left to right, then through the bottom shed from right to left. Rock the cards. Move the weft back through the bottom shed from left to right and through the top shed from right to left. Repeat until you reach the desired length.

Combining connected double strip card weaving with regular card weaving creates a pocket. (Photo, S. Rawlings)

c) *Tubular*

You can create a tubular fabric by using a single weft to connect both sides of a double strip of weaving.

TUBULAR

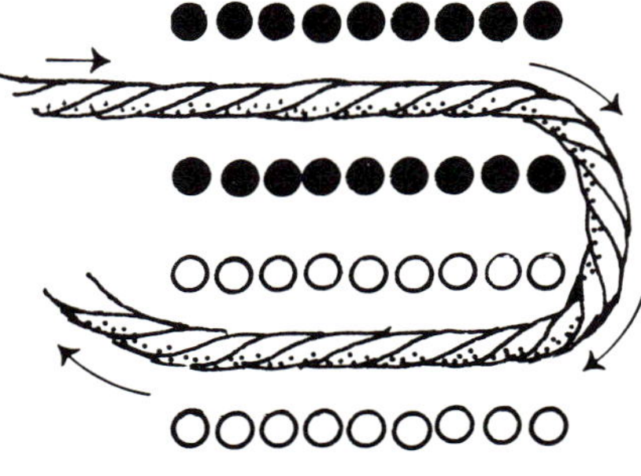

Insert the weft left to right through the top shed, then right to left through the bottom shed. Rock the cards and repeat the process.

Tubular fabric which has been stuffed with cotton. (Photo, S. Rawlings)

d) *Double Cloth*

If, instead of rocking the cards back and forth, you turn them two or more quarter turns in the same direction and insert a separate weft into the sheds after each turn, you will cause the upper and lower warp threads to interlock. The result is a single woven band called double cloth.

Traditionally, this turning method is used in conjunction with rocking the cards to form characteristic block letters or geometric block-like designs in the weaving. This is done first by threading the cards with only two colors, one for holes A and B, the other for holes C and D.

Start by rocking the cards between positions 1 and 2 and insert a separate weft into each shed after every change of position. To bring the second color to the surface and thereby weave a pattern, move some of the cards, independent of the rest of the pack, two quarter turns in the same direction. Now rock all the cards together as a pack and insert the wefts. Continue rocking the pack until you again wish to change the arrangement of the two colors.

By inserting two separate wefts you will get two bands of weaving which are connected only in those places where the cards have been turned (i.e., where the pattern shows). You can connect the bands along the edges as well, however, if you insert the weft following the instructions for making a tubular fabric with the cards in the diamond position (c on opposite page).

This is an example of double cloth which has been woven with the cards in a diamond position.

6. CHANGING THE METHOD OF INSERTING THE WEFT

It is possible to create a tubular fabric by inserting the weft from the same side only. To do this, you must run the inserted weft back under the woven band to be inserted again from the same side. Once you reach the desired length, draw the two sides of the band together by tightening the weft. This method of creating a tubular fabric enables you to weave a more intricate pattern into the tube than does the diamond position technique. (5 above).

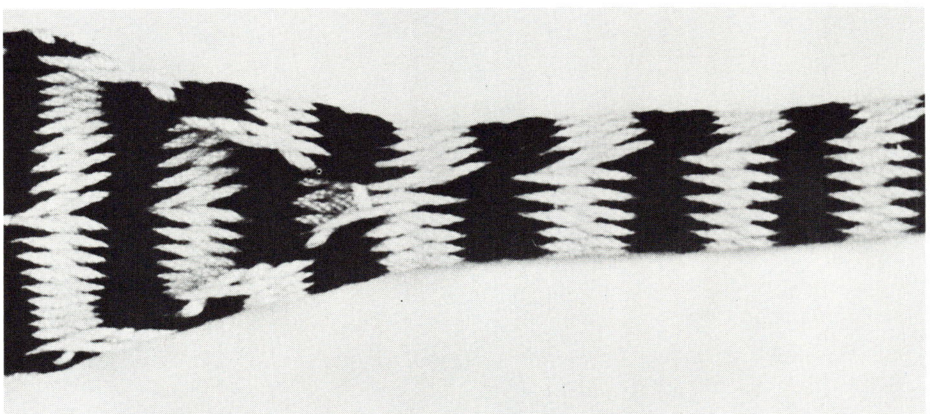

To weave a tubular fabric, draw both sides of the band together by tightening the weft.

"Marugawa." Kay Sekimachi. Linen. These tubular sculptures were created by inserting the weft from the same side. The tubes are an average of 5' long and each was woven with approximately 78 cards. (Photo, Lance Hughston)

7. EXTENDING THE WEFT BEYOND THE WARP

Instead of pulling the weft taut after each insertion through the shed so that it forms a uniform edge on the band, you can extend it several inches (or whatever length you wish) beyond one side of the warp threads. This will produce loops of free hanging weft thread which can be used in many interesting ways.

Here the extended wefts are knotted and form decorative fringe along the full length of one side of the band.

A single card woven band serves as the tie as well as trim for this hat by Jackie Wollenberg. The weft was extended during the weaving of the middle section of the band. The extended weft loops were then used to make the body of the hat. (Photo, Bob Warner)

"Peacock Basket." Joan Sterrenburg. Polytwine, silk, feathers. Card weaving, crochet, embroidery, binding. (Photo, courtesy of the artist)

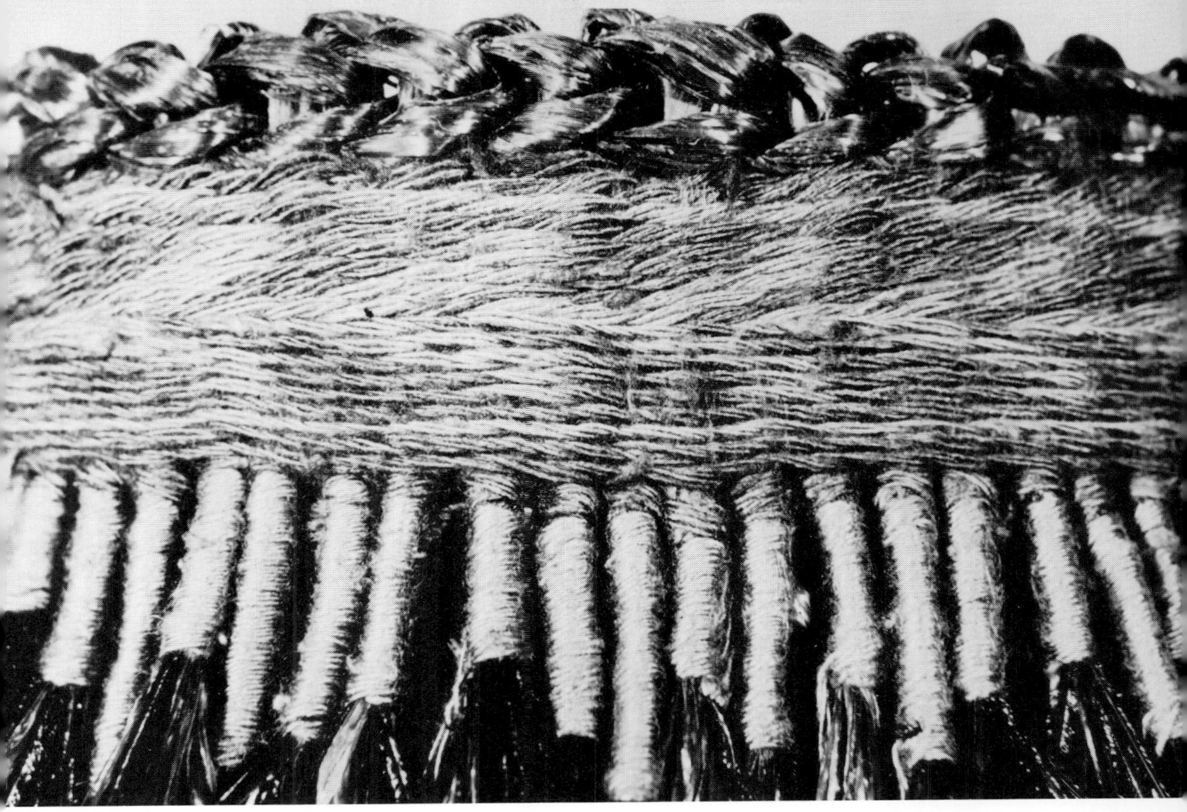

"Peacock Basket." Joan Sterrenburg. Detail. The polytwine weft of this card woven band was extended beyond the lower warp threads. Peacock flue feathers then were attached—by binding—to these extended weft threads thus creating a full ring of fringe around the neck of the basket. (Photo, courtesy of the artist)

8. ADDING AN ADDITIONAL WEFT

One way in which you can create weft interest in the traditionally warp-faced fabric produced by card weaving is to add an additional weft. There are many inventive ways to do this including the following.

If you work the extra weft over and under the top warp threads, you will create a brocaded effect. Shiny rattail is the extra weft in this mercerized cotton band. (Photo, S. Rawlings)

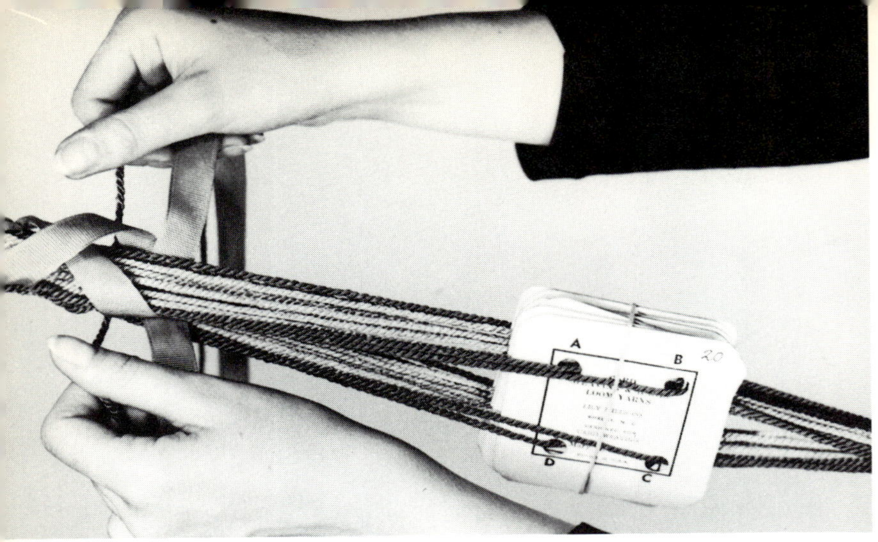

Here, the ends of a piece of ribbon, the extra weft, are criss-crossed over and under the upper warp threads.

Untitled Hanging. Helene Durbin. Wool, peacock feathers. In each of the five card woven strips of this hanging, the additional weft is a peacock's feather which has been woven in tandem with the original weft. (Photo, Bob Warner)

9. MOVING THE CARDS SIDEWAYS

Because of the flexibility of the card weaving setup, it is possible to pick up a group of threaded cards and insert them back into the pack in a different position. By shuffling the cards and thus the color arrangement of the warp threads in this way, you automatically alter the pattern of the band. You can also move one or more groups of cards over and under each other several times to braid the warp threads before continuing to weave.

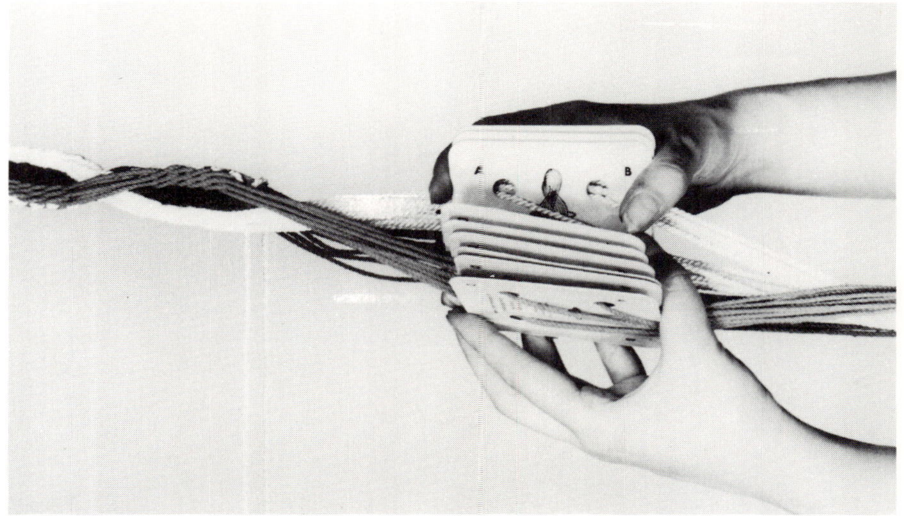

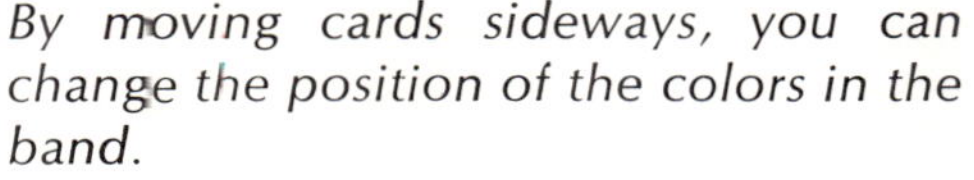

By moving cards sideways, you can change the position of the colors in the band.

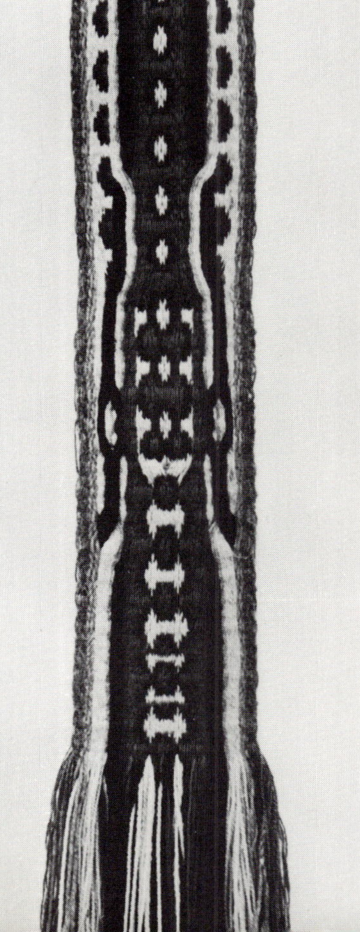

Untitled Hanging. Helene Durbin. Wool. Groups of cards were moved sideways to change the pattern in this piece. (Photo, S. Rawlings)

10. DIVIDING THE CARDS INTO TWO OR MORE GROUPS AND WEAVING EACH SEPARATELY

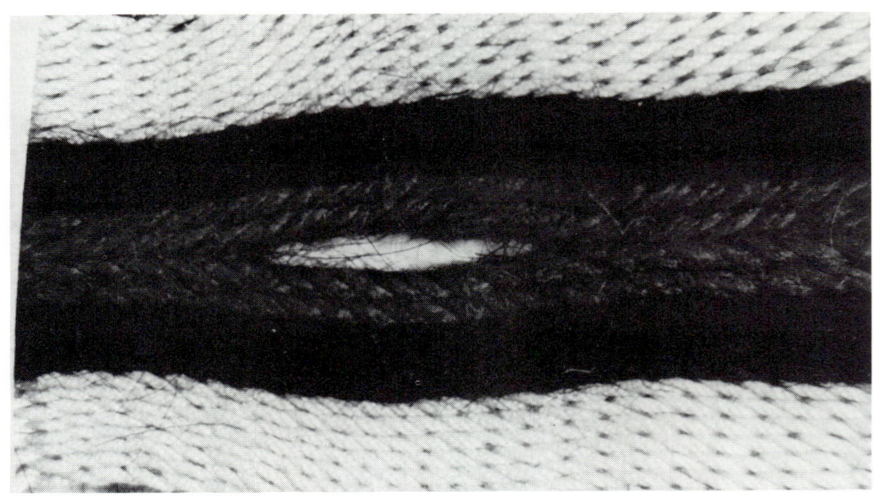

You can make a slit in the band by dividing the cards into two groups, weaving each group separately for as long as you would like the slit to be and then reuniting the cards and weaving with them as one group once again. It is also possible and effective to divide the cards into more than two groups to create several slits.

Space Divider. Dorothy Field. Detail. Sisal, tarred marlin. This netting effect is the result of dividing the cards into several small groups, weaving each group separately, then splitting each group of cards in half and combining one half of one group with half the cards of an adjacent group, thus creating new separate small groups of cards to be woven individually. As many wefts as there are groups of cards are used and the same wefts are extended to each new group of cards. (Photo, Rudy vander Vegt)

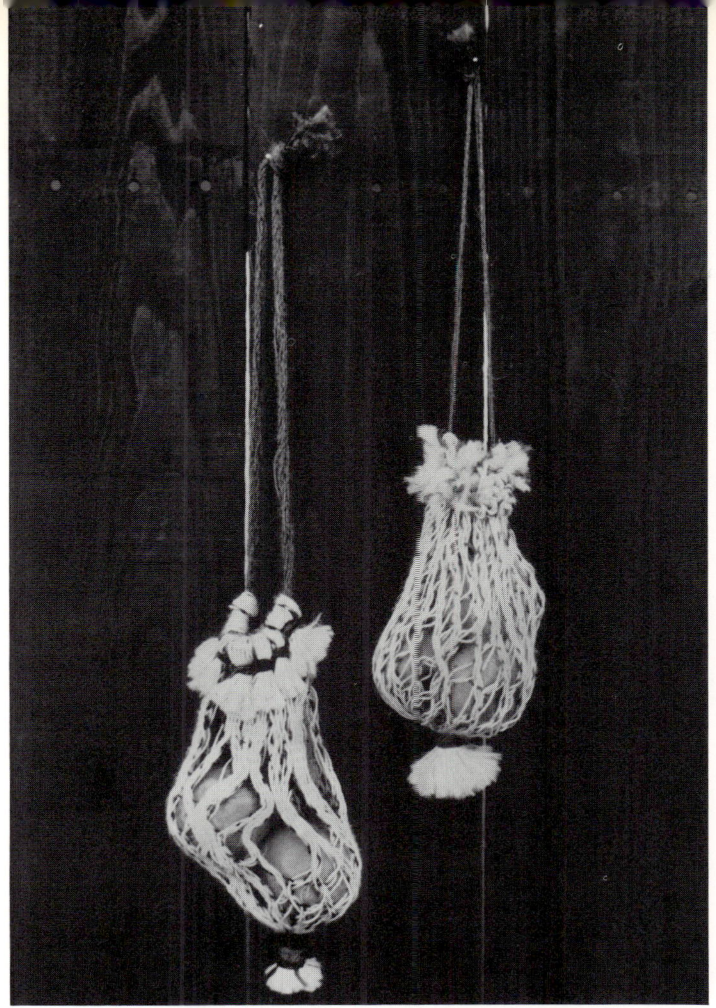

Fruit bags. Dorothy Field. Mohair. (Photo, Rudy vander Vegt)

Tent. Dorothy Field. Wool, sisal. (Photo, Rudy vander Vegt)

11. CHANGING THE THREADING

You can achieve various textural effects, both subtle and bold, simply by changing the threading of the cards.

Three-Hole Threading Instead of threading all four holes of each card, you can thread only three holes. Every time the empty hole appears in the key hole position (upper left-hand corner) while weaving, an indentation will appear on the surface of the fabric. Thus, by changing the position of the empty hole from card to card, you can weave various patterns in relief. The fabric produced by this type of threading is, of course, three-ply rather than the normal four-ply.

Fabric with a diagonal relief pattern. (Photo, S. Rawlings)

Two-Hole Threading You can thread two consecutive holes or two diagonal holes of the cards. Either way, you will get a two-ply fabric.

Consecutive Holes If two holes on the same side of each card are threaded, you will get not only a relief effect like that produced by three-hole threading but also weft interest in the fabric. Every time each of the two empty holes appears in the key hole position while weaving, the weft will show on the surface of the band. If the weft is the same color and texture as the warp, the effect will be subtle; however, a different colored weft could result in a weft-dominated pattern.

Two-hole threading and a dark weft thread were used for this band to create a weft-dominated pattern. (Photo, S. Rawlings)

Diagonal Holes You can thread either set of diagonal holes on the card. If you thread all the cards alike and turn them in the same direction throughout the weaving, you will get the normal twisted warp-faced fabric. If, however, you alternate between two quarter turns in one direction and two quarter turns in reverse, the fabric will be in plain weave.

If you alternate the threading diagonal for each card, you will get a fabric with a staggered or irregular "stitch" effect as opposed to the even rows of "stitches" produced by cards in which the same diagonal holes have been threaded.

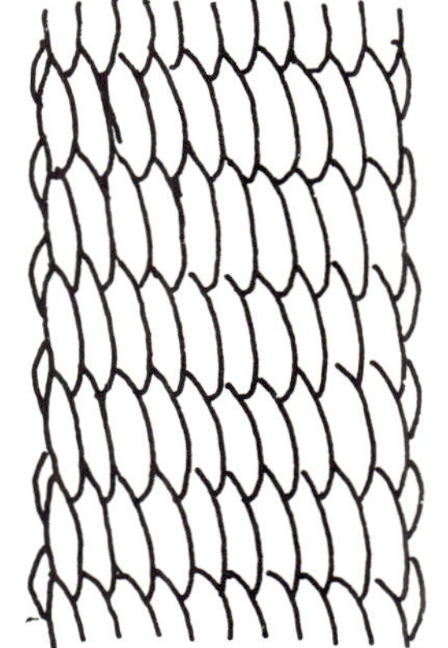

Two-hole diagonal threading—twisted warp.

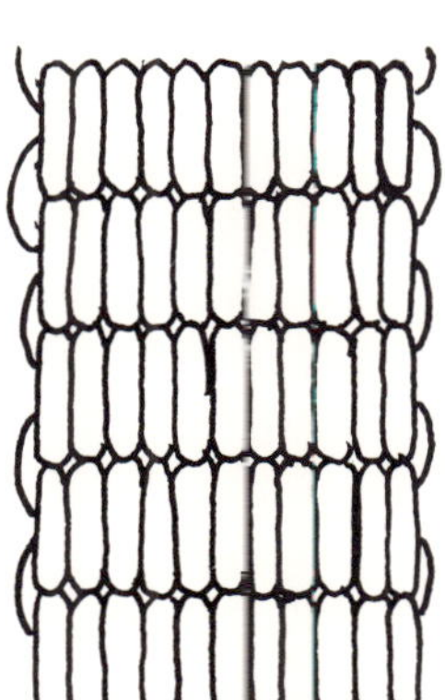

Two-hole diagonal threading—plain weave.

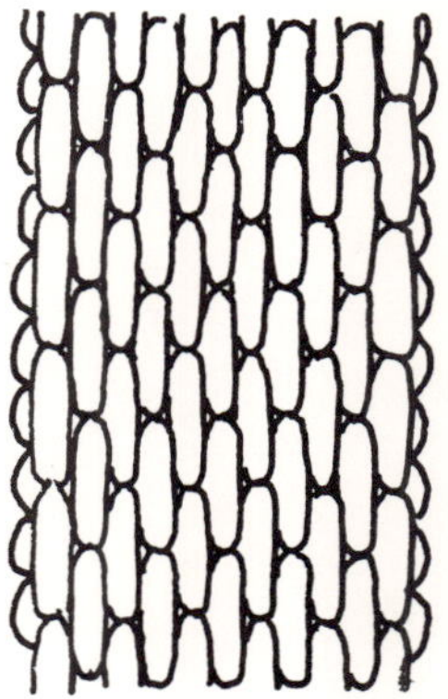

Alternate two-hole diagonal threading.

An effective way to take advantage of the two-ply nature of fabric produced by two-hole threading is to weave with a weft thread much thicker and heavier than the warp threads. Although the weft is covered by the warp in the finished piece, it is covered by only one layer or ply of warp instead of the usual two. Consequently, the outline of the exaggerated weft shows through the warp more sharply than it otherwise would and creates a textural pattern in the band.

"Day of the Axolotl." Jean Singerman. Ikat silk, synthetic yarns. Card weaving and loom weaving. (Photo, courtesy of the artist)

"Day of the Axolotl." Jean Singerman. Detail. (Photo, courtesy of the artist)

Two-Hole and Four-Hole Threading If you use cards with two-hole threading in combination with cards with four-hole threading, the surface of the fabric will be characterized by large and small "stitches."

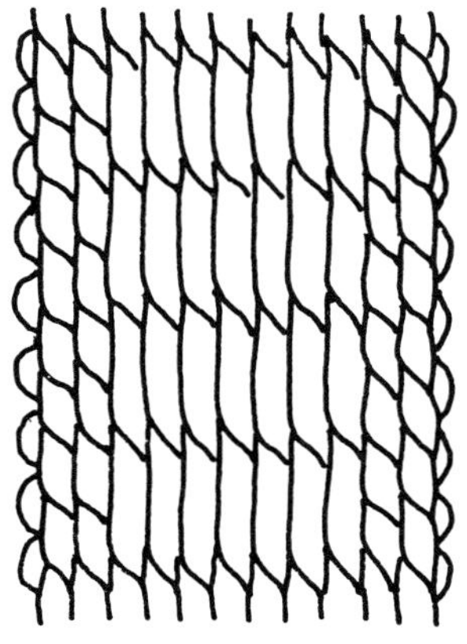

Four-hole threading was used for the two outer cards on each side of this band and two-hole threading for all the cards in between. Each four-hole threaded card produced a small "stitch" and every two-hole threaded card a large "stitch" twice as long as the smaller one.

Multiple Threads per Hole Threading more than one warp thread in each hole of the cards adds thickness to the band. Therefore, if you thread some holes with only one thread and others with varying numbers of warp threads, you will add dimensional interest.

12. ADDING OR ELIMINATING CARDS

It is possible to widen a band by adding threaded cards either on the sides or within the pack.

Cape. Maria Elena Arejula. Black chenille. The weaver started the neck of the cape with 25 cards and finished up the bottom and widest part with 250 cards. The collar, border, and lining are of black satin. (Photo, Sing-Si Schwartz)

You can also narrow a band by eliminating cards.

"Blue Card Weaving." Phoebe McAfee. This hanging was woven to a point by eliminating cards. (Photo, Sol Columbus)

13. USING CARDS WITH MORE THAN FOUR HOLES

You will be able to weave more intricate patterns by using cards with more than four holes.

Some cards contain a center hole which can be threaded with an extra warp thread (usually a strong cord) to add strength to the band. This extra warp thread will not show in the surface of the band. (Photo, S. Rawlings)

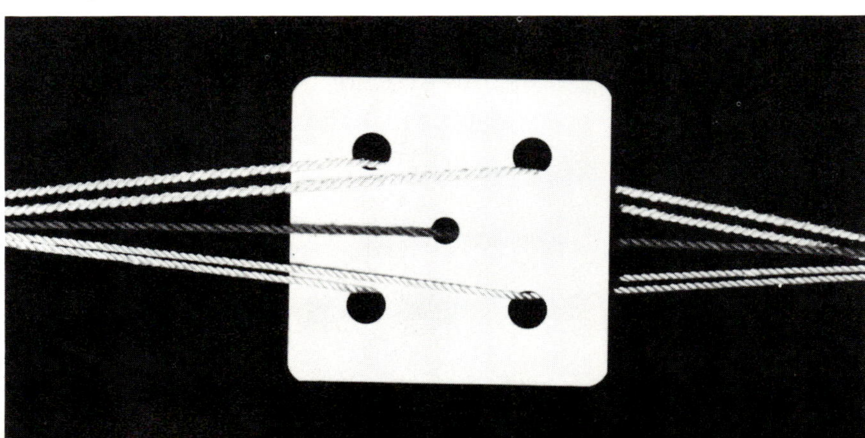

Hexagonal cards are fairly common. The two extra corner holes give you two more lines (E and F) to work with on the pattern draft. Weaving by Jackie Wollenberg. (Photo, Bob Warner)

14. SETTING UP THE CARDS ON A FRAME

You can work with many more cards than it is convenient to hold if you set up the cards on either a simple wooden frame which you can buy or make yourself or a regular frame loom. Working this way, you will be able to make wide as well as narrow bands. It is also possible to do card weaving and regular loom weaving at the same time, using one weft to weave across the regular warp as well as the warp threads of the cards.

Cards set up on a regular loom. Mary Anne Mauro. (Photo, Jim Mauro)

"The Egyptian." Mary Anne Mauro. Rug wool. (Photo, Jim Mauro)

CHAPTER 7

WHAT TO MAKE

You can make practically any article of clothing or dress accessory out of card woven bands including stylish belts, suspenders, watchbands, purses, jewelry, hats, vests, even colorful laces for ski boots or hiking shoes. The kind of thread fiber you use determines whether the article is dressy or casual—the shinier fibers such as silk and rayon tend to dress up a piece.

Because of the strength and variety of card woven fabric, the technique also lends itself to a wide assortment of functional and decorative items for the home, the office, and the playing field. Pillows, blankets, screen dividers, plant holders, pencil or glasses cases, and trim for tennis racket covers or golf club bags are just a few of the multitude of ways to add flair with card weaving. And again, by changing the type of fiber, you can vary the style of the weaving to suit the taste and mood of any home or individual. You can also add beads, shells, buttons, bells, feathers—whatever strikes you—to accent your weavings. (The thick, long fringes of much card weaving make excellent anchor cords for these decorative additions.)

The following presents directions for specific projects as well as what we hope will be inspirations for projects of your own invention and interpretation. Ideas are all around you. If an article can be made out of any sort of natural or synthetic fabric—cloth, leather, plastic sheets and so forth—it probably can be card woven.

PROJECTS FOR HER

Belts make good beginning projects. Each of the following patterns can be made up in just a couple of hours. The amount of thread needed for the following patterns varies from individual to individual according to the waist measurement. To figure how long to cut the weft and warp threads, follow the formula given in Chapter 4. Note the different ways you can finish the warp ends to change the method of fastening the belt.

◄
"The Sea." Phoebe McAfee. 20" x 27". Persian wool. The artist used 200 cards set up on a regular loom to make this weaving which has been mounted on a piece of driftwood. Decorative glass beads have been added to the fringe. (Photo, Sol Columbus)

Belt. Sally Specht. Rayon slide cord, hat straw. (Photo, S. Rawlings)

Belt. Sally Specht. Rayon slide cord (black and green). Additional weft—hat straw (red and black).

Pattern:

	1	2	3	4	5	6	7	8	9	10	11	12
A	black	black	black	black	green	green	green	green	black	black	black	black
B	black	black	black	black	green	green	green	green	black	black	black	black
C	black	black	black	black	green	green	green	green	black	black	black	black
D	black	black	black	black	green	green	green	green	black	black	black	black
	/	/	/	/	/	/	\	\	\	\	\	\

colors: black (shaded square); green (empty square)

turning: counterclockwise throughout
double weft method

Weave the belt to the required waist measurement. Allow 26" for fringe on both ends and tie a knot in each fringe thread to prevent fraying. Start the additional red weft in the fourth shed and thereafter insert it every four sheds in the double weft method to make it criss-cross over the top of the warp. Insert the black additional weft one shed after the red. Tie off both additional wefts inside the shed and cut off any extra hat straw. This way the knot will be hidden by the warp threads.

Belt. Sally Specht. Rayon slide cord (green and yellow)
(Photo, S. Rawlings)

Pattern:

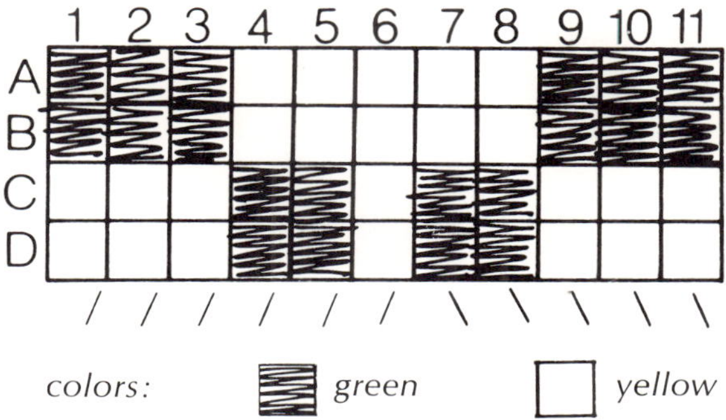

turning: counterclockwise throughout
double weft method

Thread the cards so that the warp threads loop around the ring as shown. (You can use two rings if you prefer.)
Weave the belt to the correct waist measurement. Tie a knot in each fringe thread to prevent fraying. (The fringe is 24" long on each end.)

Belt. Sally Specht. (Photo, S. Rawlings)
Materials: White cotton cording. Additional weft—1" wide grosgrain ribbon (red) and ¼" wide grosgrain ribbon (blue). Cut the ribbon twice as long as the waist measurement plus 4".
Pattern: Use ten cards. Thread each card with the cotton cording warp threads—half (╲) and half (╱). Turn the cards in the same direction throughout the weaving. Use the double weft method. A finer thread than the warp cording can be used for the weft.
Use the two ribbons separately as additional wefts and in the double weft method. Start the wider ribbon in the first shed along with the regular weft and thereafter insert both ends of the ribbon every seven sheds. Start the narrow ribbon in the second shed and thereafter insert it one shed after the wider ribbon. The ribbons thus form a crisscross pattern on the surface of the belt.

When you have woven the band almost to the desired length, use a square knot to tie the ends of the wider ribbon together inside the shed. Cut off any extra ribbon. Turn the cards a quarter turn and do the same for the narrower ribbon. Continue weaving with the cotton cording weft until you reach the desired length of the band.

To add interest to the loosely hanging warp threads that form a fringe, tie knots at various points in some of the threads and then tie small lengths of the narrow ribbon right above the knots. (The knots act as anchors and prevent the ribbons from sliding downward.)

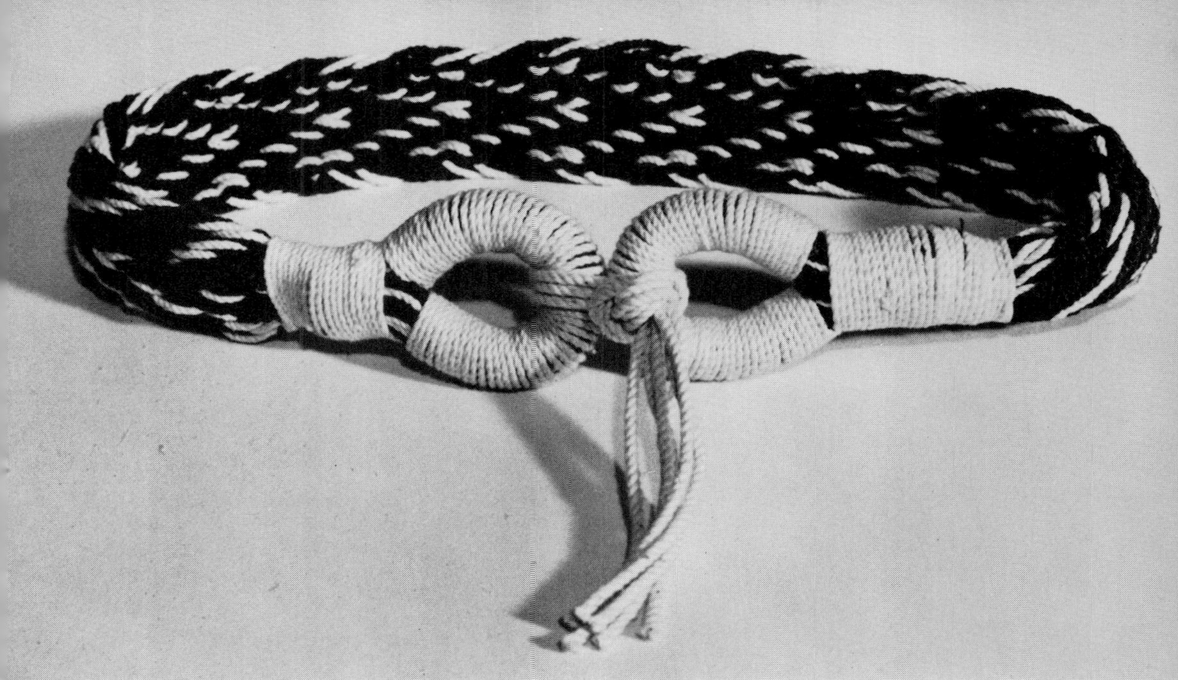

Belt. Sally Specht. (Photo, S. Rawlings.)
Materials: Rayon slide cord (blue and white).

Pattern:

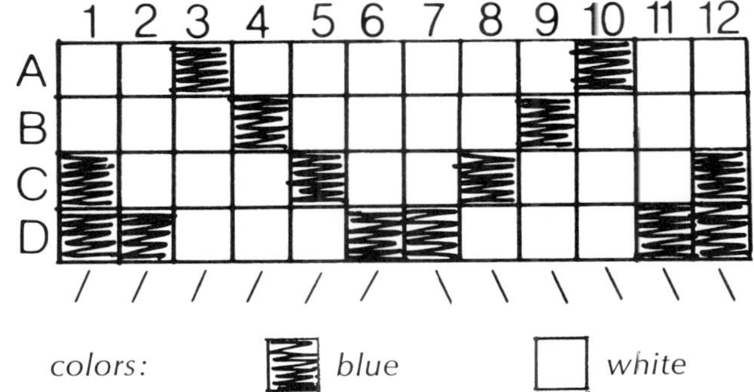

turning: counterclockwise throughout; two quarter turns before inserting the weft
double weft method

Weave the belt to the correct waist measurement less 4½" for each wrapped eyelet. To achieve the eyelet effect, you must use the white cotton cording to wrap around the fringe on each end of the belt.

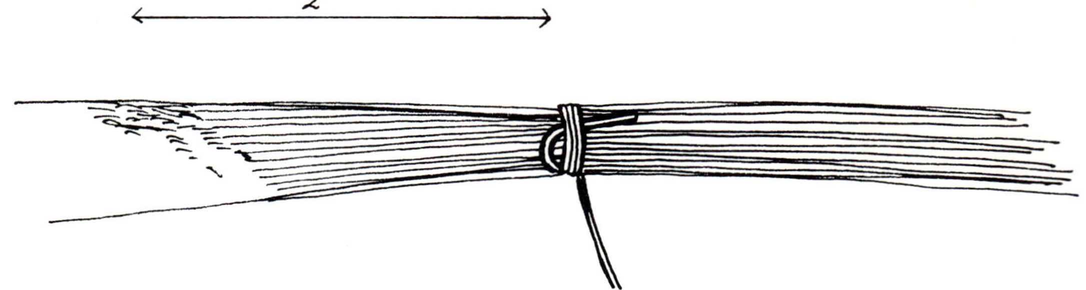

Begin the wrapping 2" from the end of the finished weaving.

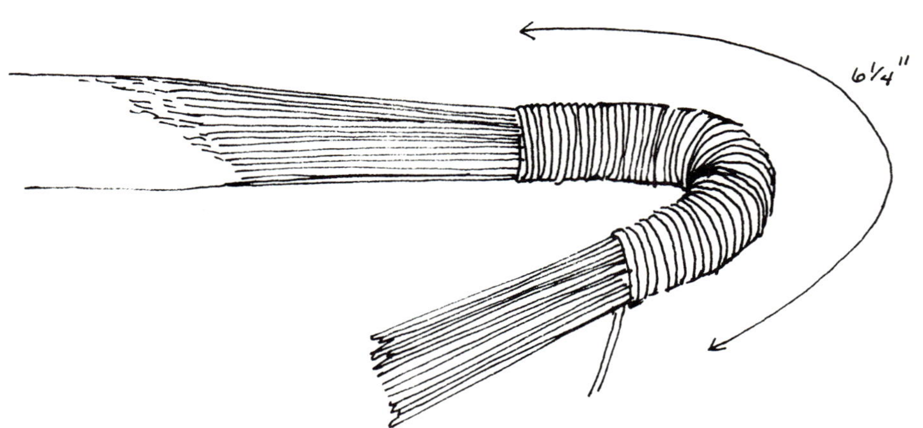

Wrap enough fringe to fold back into an eyelet.

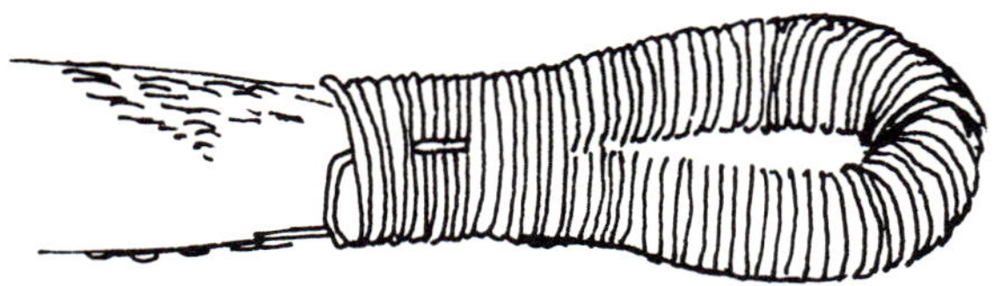

Secure the eyelet by wrapping as shown.

Vest. Sally Specht. (Photo, S. Rawlings)
Materials: Two-ply Persian rug yarn (shocking pink, ultramarine blue, red)
Wide strip: 34 cards threaded ½ (╲); ½ (╱).
Narrow strip: 18 cards threaded ½ (╲); ½ (╱).
Pattern: Any number of pattern designs of your own invention would work well for the bands in this piece.

To make the vest, hand-stitch together card woven bands according to the diagram.

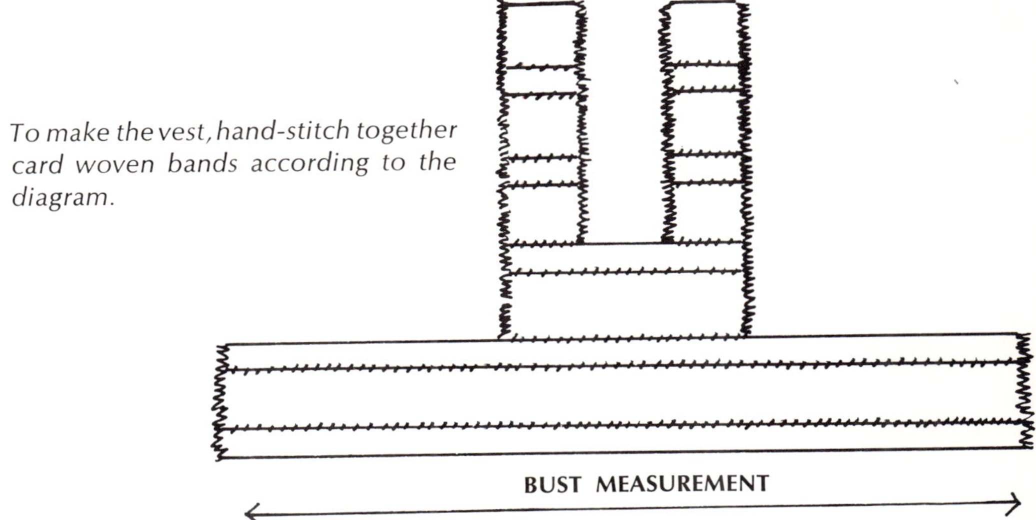

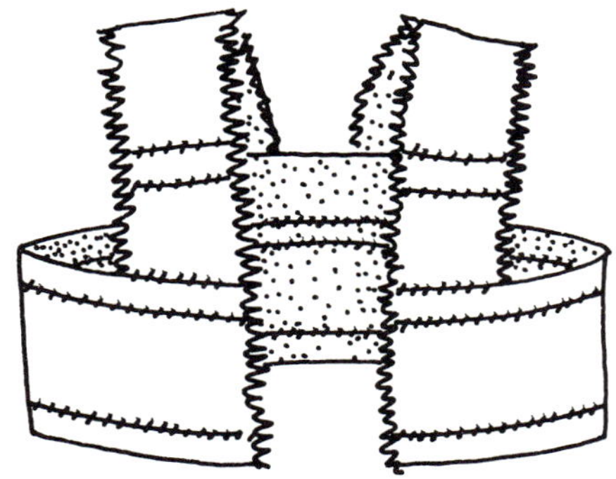

Stitch the straps to the front to complete the vest.
Make the tassels separately and sew them on the vest after it has been put together. Steam the fringe along the edges to make it fluffy.

Glasses case. Susan Lehman. (Photo, S. Rawlings) Persian wool (32 cards). This is one card woven strip 18" long which has been folded over front to back and hand-sewn on the side seams, creating a pouch long enough to hold a pair of glasses. One end of the strip was hemmed by machine. Two decorative rows of chain stitch embroidery cover the machine stitching. The other end of the strip which forms the flap was finished with tassels. The tassels were made by twisting two groups of warp threads together tightly in one direction and then, in turn, twisting two or more of these groups together in the opposite direction creating a candy cane striped effect. Each tassel was finished with an overhand knot.

Headband. Mike Wollenberg. (Photo, Bob Warner)

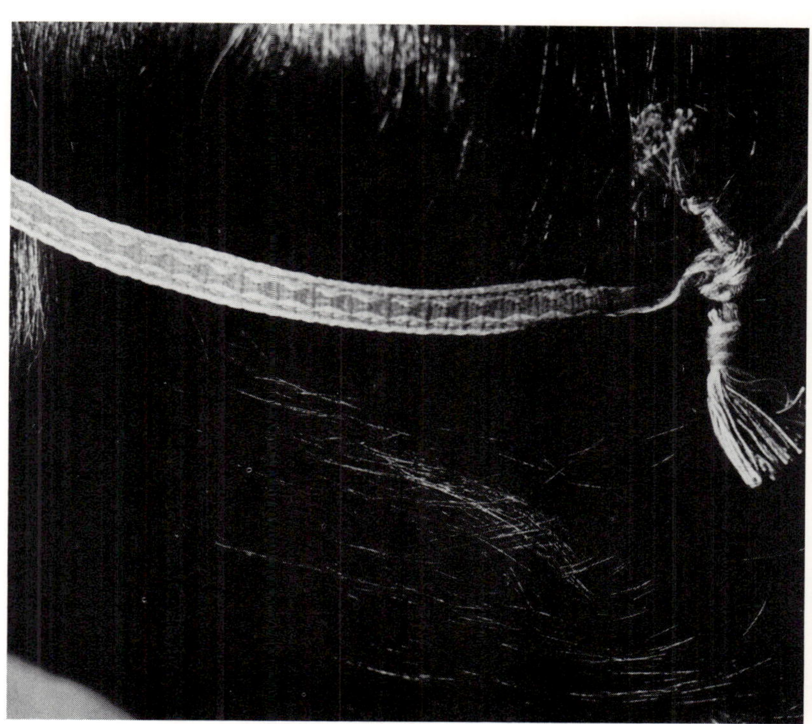

Mercerized cotton. Thirty cards were used to make this delicately patterned band. An overhand knot was tied in each end of the band to secure the weaving. (Photo, Bob Warner)

Shoulder bag. Jean Singerman. Ikat wool. Card woven strips sewn together. (Photo, Bob Warner)

Sandal. Sally Specht. Rayon slide cord and nylon cording. Eight cards were used to weave a 15" strap for this sandal. (Photo, S. Rawlings)

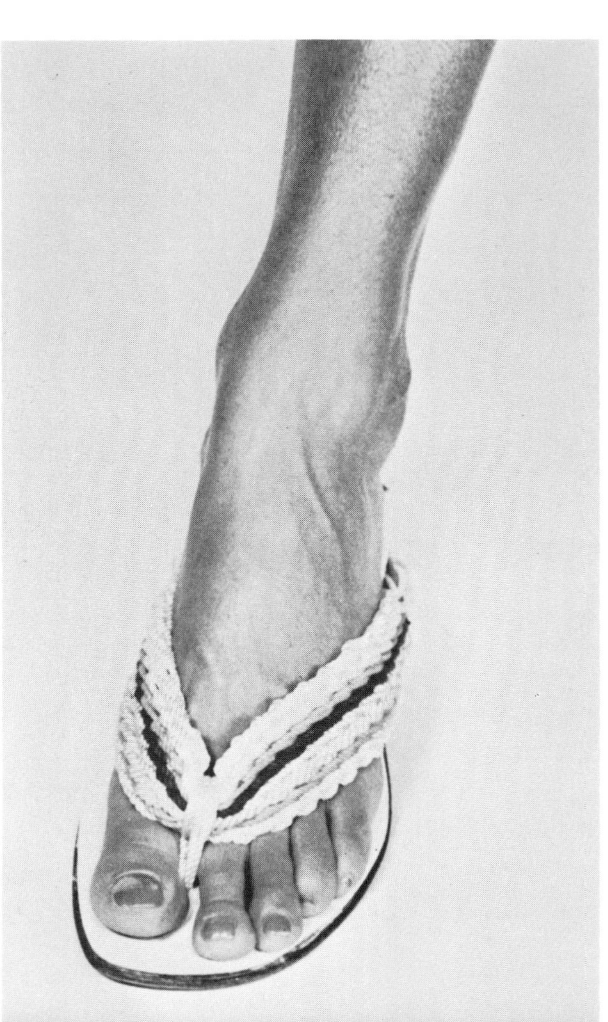

Poncho. Jackie Wollenberg. (Photo, Bob Warner) Swedish matte two-ply and four-ply yarn. Seventeen bands were sewn together by hand to make this rectangular poncho. An average of 24 cards per band was used and each band was prepatterned (i.e., the pattern was drafted out on paper before weaving). Two- and three-hole threadings were used for six of the bands and four-hole threadings for the rest. The direction of threading was varied and the cards were turned in both directions. The neck opening was made by cutting the middle band in half and sewing back each end. (Another way to make the opening in ponchos is to use an even number of bands and leave an unsewn space between the middle two bands big enough to allow your head to fit through it.)

Necklace. Betty Morris. (Photo, S. Rawlings) Wool (18 cards). The neck opening was made by dividing the cards in half and weaving each group of cards separately (see p. 54). The slit is 11½" long; the entire necklace 32" long. Shells have been tied onto the fringe.

Poncho. Jackie Wollenberg. Detail. (Photo, Bob Warner)

Cat collar. Sally Specht. (Photo, S. Rawlings)
Materials: Cotton cording (red, orange, blue).

Cat collar. Sally Specht.

Cat collar Pattern:

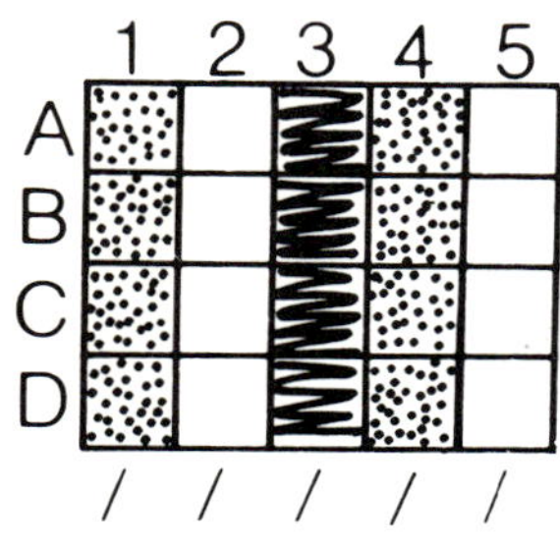

Thread the cards so that the warp threads loop around the crossbar in the middle of the buckle. You do this just as you do for the belt buckle shown on page 36. Weave for about an inch and add the metal loop. The loop holds the fringed end of the collar in place when being worn and can be used to attach a leash. To secure the loop to the collar, remove the top two threads from each card. Insert these threads through the metal loop and rethread them in the cards. Weave until the collar measures 12" from the top of the buckle. Finish the collar with a 1½" fringe.

colors: red, orange, blue

turning: counterclockwise throughout
double weft method

PROJECTS FOR HIM

Hatband. Sally Specht. (Photo, S. Rawlings)
Materials: Mercerized cotton (off-white), horsehair (black), wool (green). Use yarns which are approximately the same thickness.

Hatband Pattern:

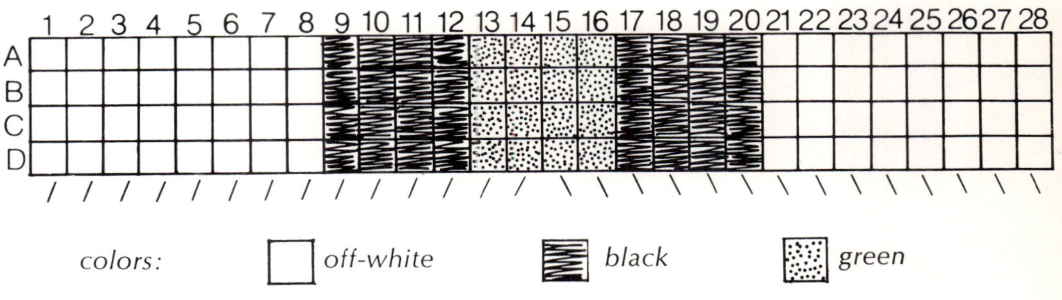

turning: counterclockwise throughout
single weft method

Measure the base of the crown of your hat. Weave the band to that measurement plus ½" for overlap. Secure the band by weaving the weft back into the last row of weaving. *(See page 36)* *Leave 1" for fringe. Place the band on the hat and hand-stitch the overlapped pieces together.*

Flag belt. Walter Seifert. Yarn—85% wool, 15% nylon (red, white, blue) (26 cards). The cards were threaded front to back and turned in a counterclockwise direction throughout the entire strip. The fringe ends were finished by twisting two groups of warp threads together tightly in one direction and then, in turn, twisting these groups together in the opposite direction. Each tassel was secured by wrapping the end.

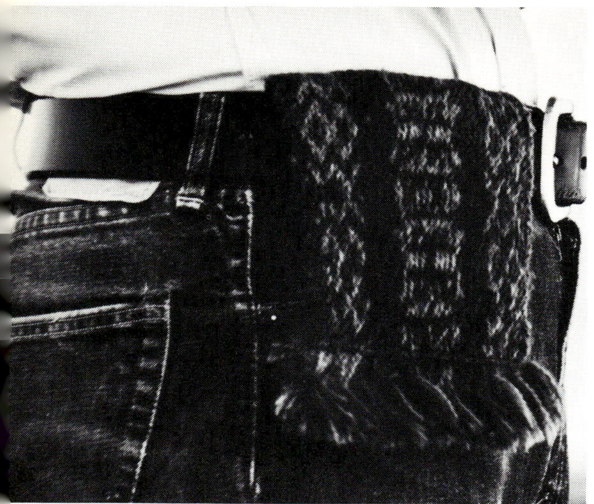

Belt pouch. Mike Wollenberg. (Photo, Bob Warner) Two-ply wool.
This flapped pouch is one card woven strip which has been folded over and hand-sewn on the sides. Seventy-four cards were used to make the strip which is 4" wide (the warp threads were drawn together tightly by the weft). The row of stitching which appears just above the fringe was made by drawing one of the outermost warp threads across the surface of the weaving and using a wrapping stitch to cover and secure it to the weaving. This is an embroidery technique called couching.

Guitar strap. Sally Specht. (Photo, Paul Christman)
Materials: Horsehair (black), jute (natural color). Felt or suede for finishing the ends of the band.

Guitar Strap Pattern:

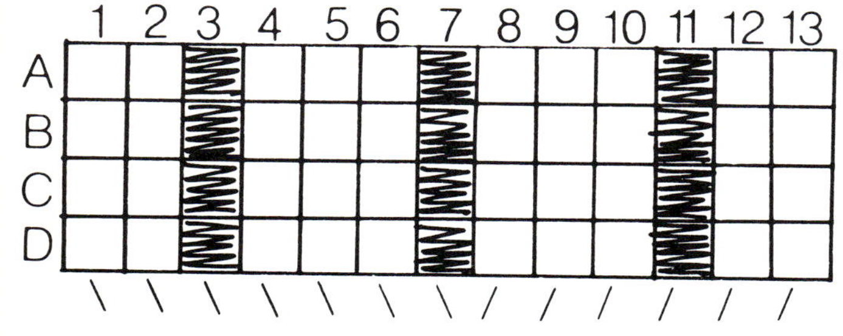

Weave the band to a length of 51". Leave a ½" fringe on each end.

colors: *black* *natural*

turning: counterclockwise throughout
single weft method—jute

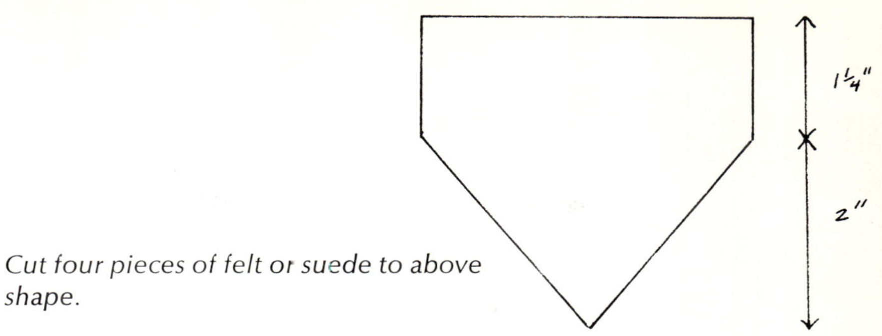

Cut four pieces of felt or suede to above shape.

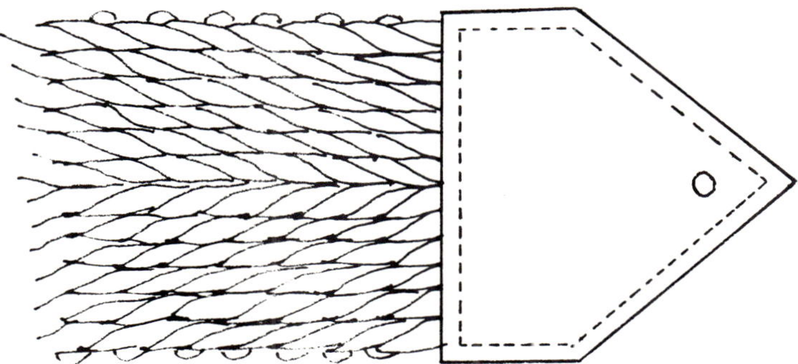

At each end of the band, machine-stitch two of the felt or suede pieces together with the ½" fringe sandwiched in between as shown.
Punch a hole in the felt or suede at each end of the strap about 1" from the point. On one end, cut a ¾" slit up from the punched hole so that the hole can fit over the end pin on the guitar. Thread the hole at the other end of the strap with another piece of cord and tie it around the neck of the guitar.

Ski or hiking boot laces. Sally Specht. (Photo, S. Rawlings) Materials: Four-ply mercerized cotton (red, green, off-white).

Laces Pattern:

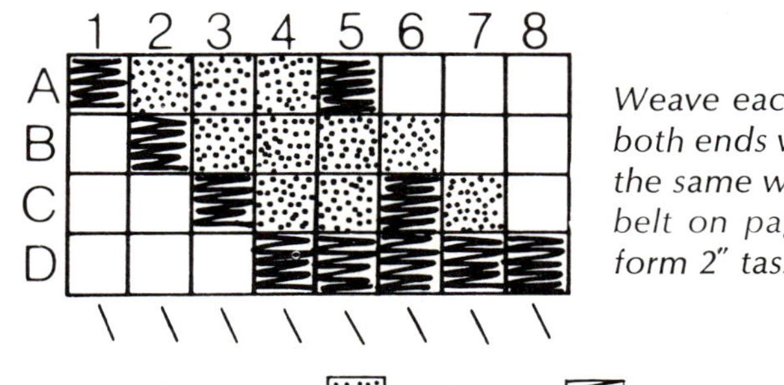

Weave each lace to a length of 77". Wrap both ends with red mercerized cotton (use the same wrapping technique used for the belt on page 68.) Trim the warp ends to form 2" tassels.

colors: red green off-white

turning: 36 turns counterclockwise; 36 turns clockwise
single weft method

Dog collar. Sally Specht. The dog's name, "Jip," was woven into the collar. (Photo, S. Rawlings)

Materials: Wool (navy and white). (Photo, S. Rawlings)

Dog Collar Pattern:

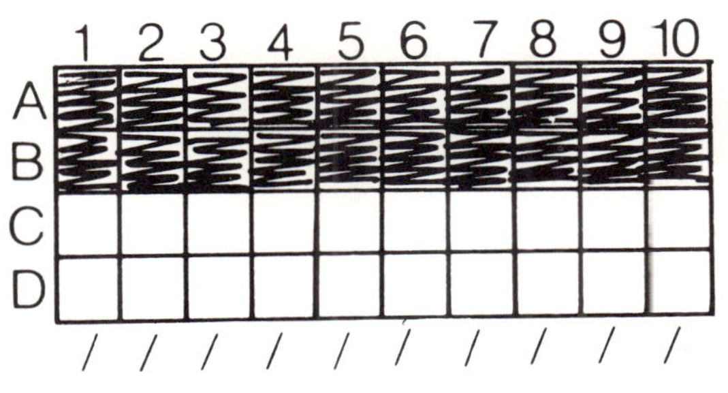

colors: navy white

turning: See Chapter 6, #5d (Weaving with the Cards in a Diamond Position—Double Cloth)

single weft method as for tubular fabric (see Chapter 6, #5c)

Thread the cards so that the warp threads loop around the crossbar in the middle of the buckle (see page 65). Weave with the cards in a diamond position until you reach the desired length, i.e., the dog's neck measurement plus 2". If you want to weave in the name of the dog as was done here, follow the instructions given in Chapter 6, #5d. Finish the collar with a 1½" long fringe.

PROJECTS FOR THE HOME

Place mat. Sally Specht. (Photo, S. Rawlings)
Materials: Spinnerin polypropylene twine (red, navy, yellow) or raffia.

Place Mat Pattern for strips 1 and 7:

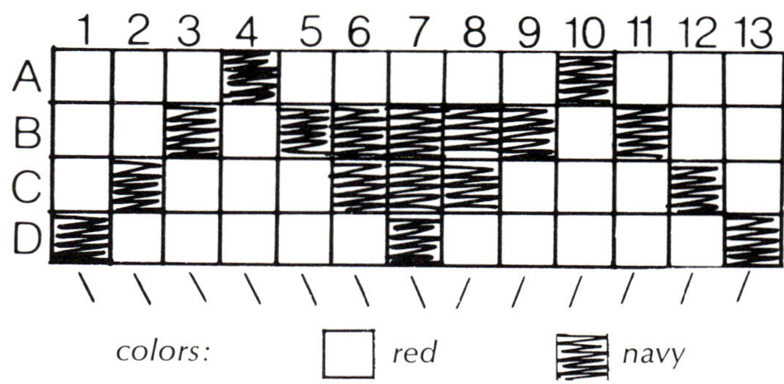

turning: counterclockwise throughout
double weft method

Place Mat Pattern for strips 2, 4, and 6:

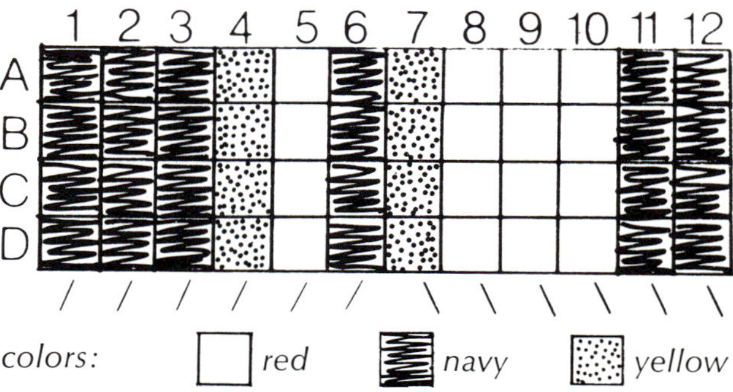

turning: counterclockwise throughout
double weft method

Place Mat Pattern for strips 3 and 5

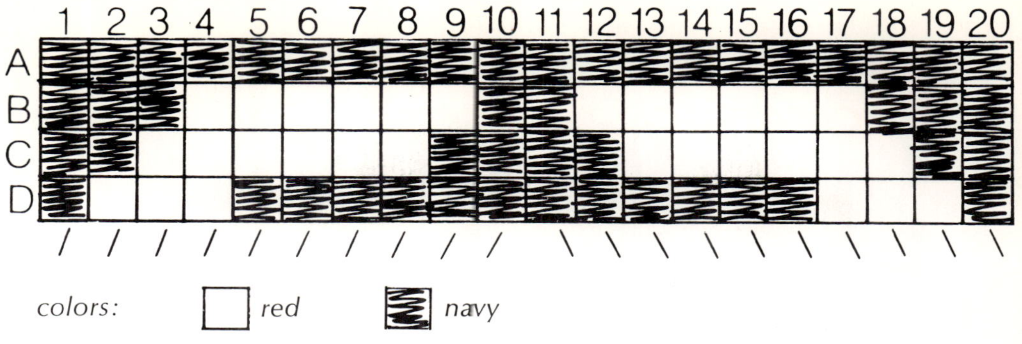

turning: counterclockwise throughout
double weft method

To make the place mat, use yellow twine to hand-sew together seven 15½″ long strips.

Napkin ring. Sally Specht. (Photo, S. Rawlings)
Materials: Mercerized cotton (white and green), wool (red)

Napkin Ring Pattern:

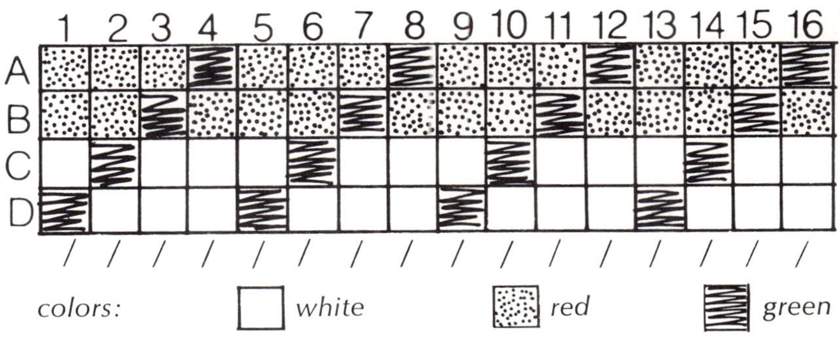

turning: counterclockwise throughout
single weft method

Weave the strip to a length of 6″. Secure the band by weaving the weft back into the last row of weaving (page 36). Leave an inch for fringe. Overlap the two ends 1¾″ including fringe and stitch them together with a decorative backstitch.

Pouch basket. Sally Specht. (Photo, S. Rawlings)
Materials: raffia (orange and green)

Pouch Basket Pattern:

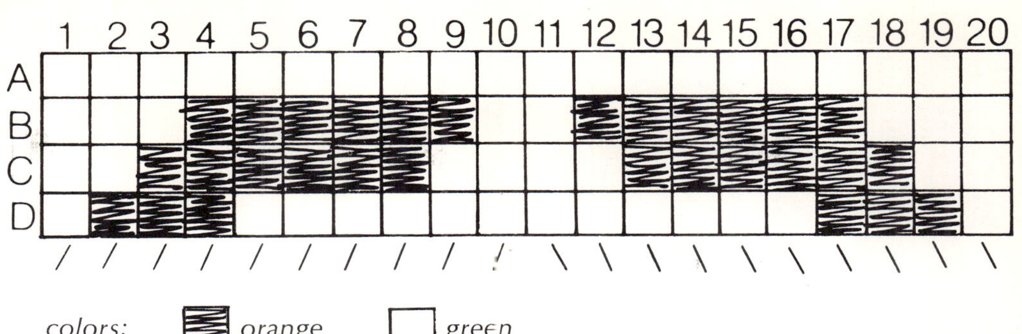

colors: orange green

turning: 4-4 cycle
double weft method

Use raffia to stitch together three card woven strips. Make each strip 15½" long including a 1¼" long fringe on one end only. Next, overlap the two ends of the newly formed wide strip so that the fringed end shows. Stitch the ends together with a backstitch. You now have a large cylinder. Stitch the bottom of the cylinder together to form a pouch. Attach leather ties to create a hanging basket.

Coaster. Sally Specht. (Photo, S. Rawlings)
Materials: Spinnerin polypropylene twine (yellow and blue) or raffia.

Coaster Pattern for strips 1, 3, 5:

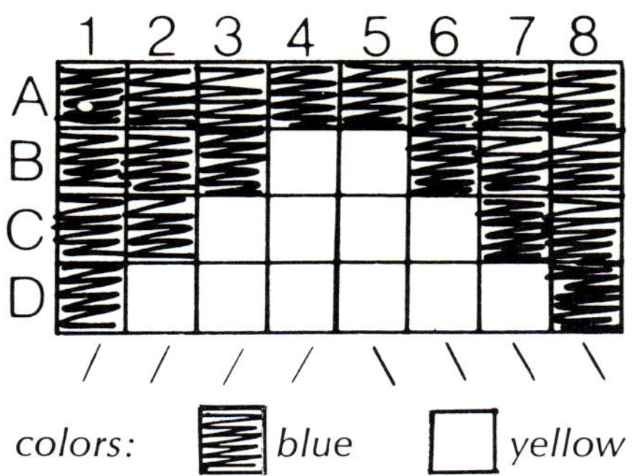

turning: counterclockwise throughout
double weft method

Coaster Pattern for strips 2 and 4:

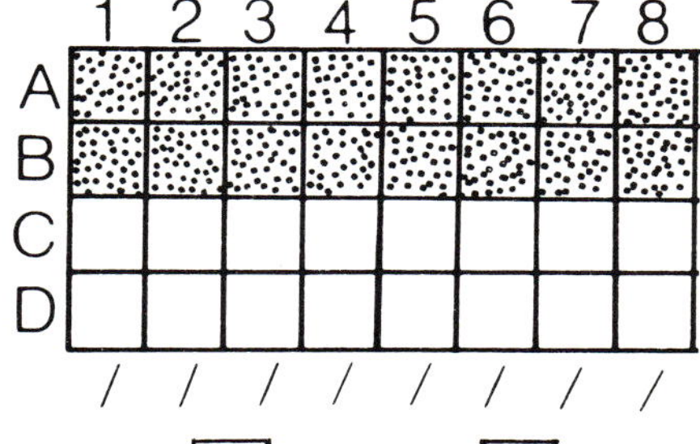

colors: orange yellow

turning: 2-2 cycle
double weft method

With twine hand-sew together five strips of card weaving, each 3¾" long, to make these coasters. Although a specific pattern is given, it is most attractive to vary pattern and colors for each coaster when making a set.

Luggage rack. Sally Specht. (Photo, Rickie Wong and Andrew Weber)
Materials: Rayon slide cord (multicolors), wool (multicolors)

Luggage Rack, Checkerboard Pattern:

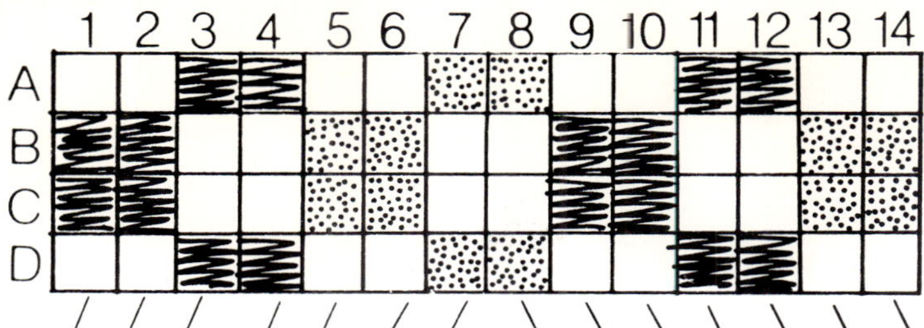

colors: The two colors of rayon slide cord used varied from band to band.
turning: counterclockwise throughout
double weft method

Luggage Rack, Striped Pattern:

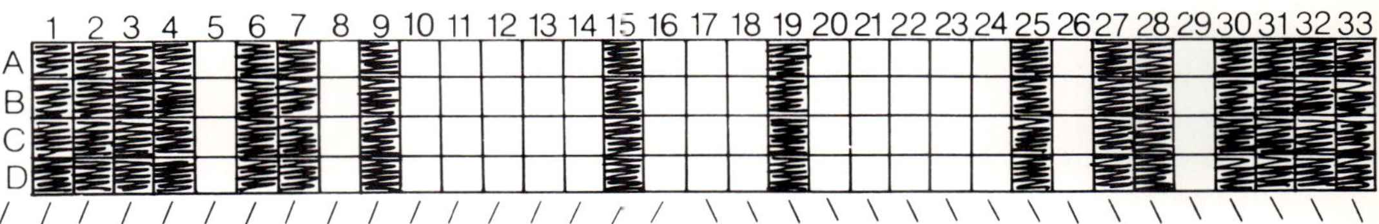

colors: The two colors of wool used varied from band to band.
turning: counterclockwise throughout
double weft method

Measure the width between the wooden crossbars on the frame of the luggage rack. Weave three strips of checkered card weaving and two strips of striped card weaving to that length adding 9" to each strip at each end for the fringe and knot. Place half of the warp ends of each strip over and the other half under the wooden crossbar and tie them together with an overhand knot. Do this on both sides of each strip with all five card woven bands to complete the luggage rack.

Hammock. Dorothy Field. (Photo, Alan La Pointe). Jute.
This 12' hammock was card woven in the netting technique (p. 54). The warp ends are secured to cow ribs which lend a graceful line to the piece.

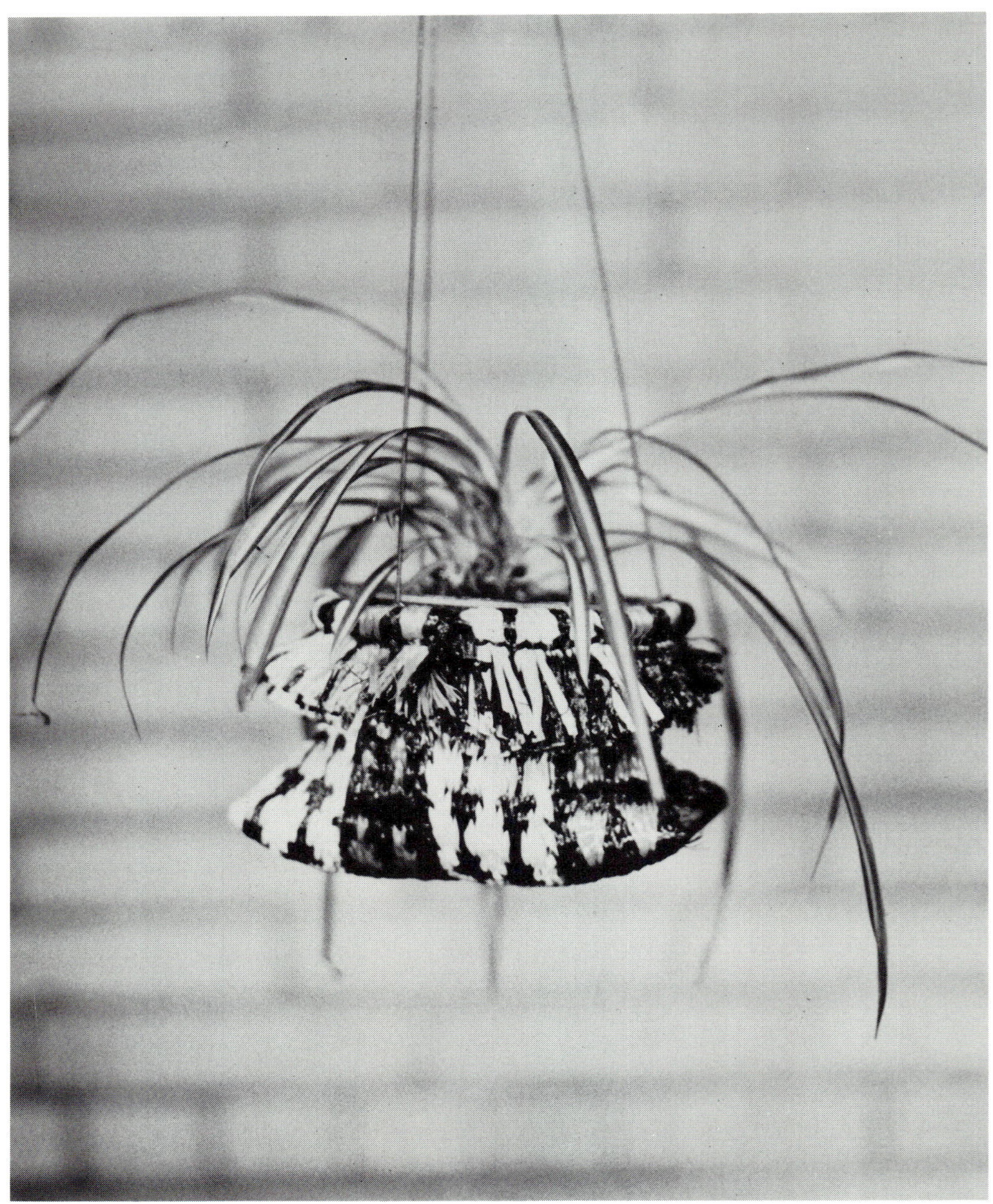

Planter. Sally Specht. (Photo, S. Rawlings)
Materials: Spinnerin polypropylene twine (red, black, white, green)

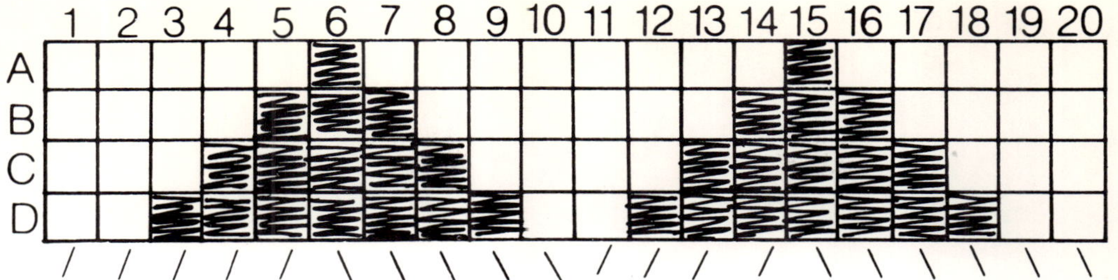

colors: Make two of the bands black and white; one band black and red; one band black and green. Use the same threading for each band.
turning: 3-3 for the two white and black strips; 4-4 for the other two strips
double weft method

Sew four card woven strips together with black raffia. Each strip should be 15½" long, of which 3" are for fringe, 1½" for each end.

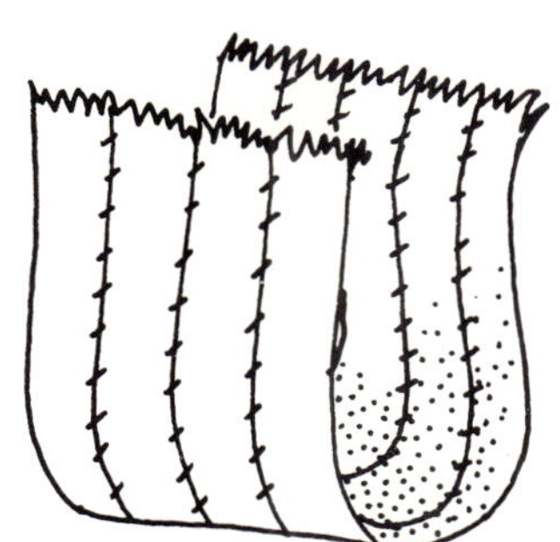

Fold each strip as shown.

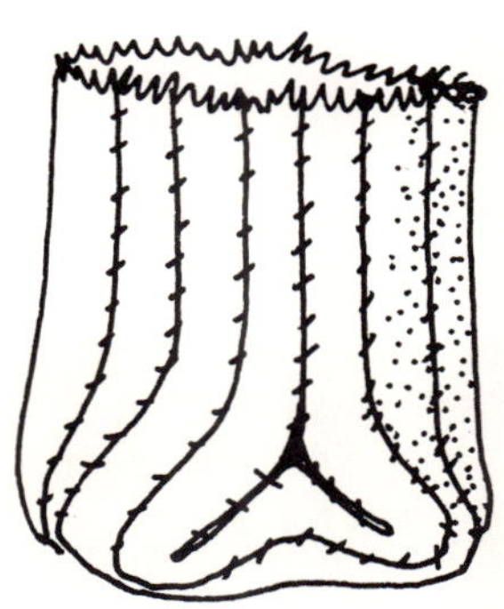

Stitch the side seams.

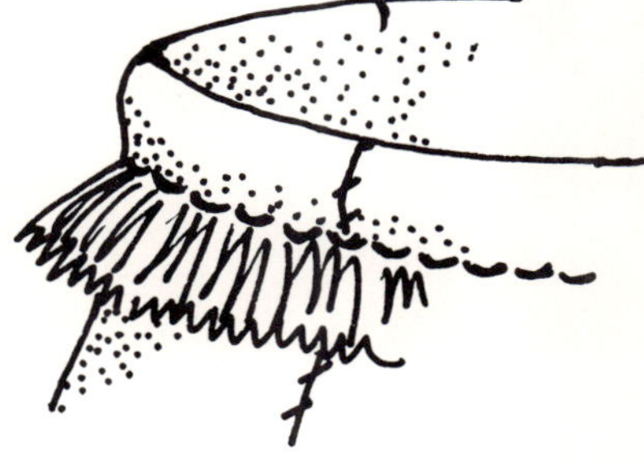

Fold the fringe down like a cuff and secure it with a backstitch.

Attach cords for hanging the basket. You can either put a ceramic flowerpot into the basket or place the plant directly in the basket. If you do the latter, it is best to fill the bottom of the basket with moss.

Basket. Maria Elena Arejula. (Photo, Kathryn McCardle) (250 cards) A wooden embroidery hoop with an 8" diameter was used as a frame for the mouth of the basket. Each warp thread was looped around and secured to the frame with a macramé knot called a Lark's Head. The cards were turned in the 4—4 cycle to weave the basket to a height of 14". The basket appears to be in plain weave because it was woven very loosely.

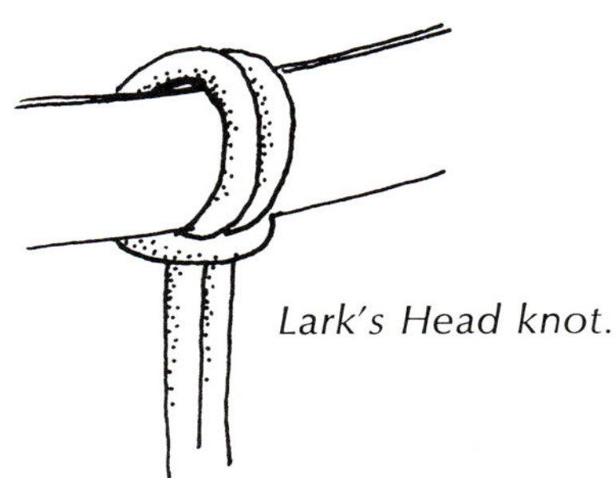

Lark's Head knot.

Basket—bottom view. Maria Elena Arejula. (Photo, Kathryn McCardle) Once the basket had been woven to the desired height, the remaining unwoven warp thread was tucked inside the basket thus adding an interesting, fluid feeling to the underside.

This piece is made of two card woven strips which have been interlaced in a basket weave and hand-stitched together. Each strip is 2½" wide and 2' long. Both ends of the strips have been woven to a point. The weaver accomplished this by starting the strip with only one card and adding on cards until she reached 18, the number of cards used for the major portion of the strip, and by finishing the other er d of the strip by eliminating cards. The cards were threaded front to back and turned clockwise throughout the weaving.

Plant mat. Maria Elena Arejula. (Photo, S. Rawlings)
Polished cable cord, cotton string.

Wall hanging. Susan Lehman. (Photo, S. Rawlings) Chenille, cotton, wool, linen, rayon bouclé, rayon.
This pictorial hanging is made of five card woven strips which have been sewn together and backed with cloth.

Materials: different weights of tie-dyed chenille and cotton yarn
Turning: clockwise and counterclockwise according to the thread color which the weaver wanted showing on the fabric surface and not according to a predetermined pattern.
The patterns for the other three strips were drafted out on paper before the weaving was started.
Houses (24 cards)
Materials: linen, rayon, cotton
Turning: four clockwise, four counterclockwise.
Fence (30 cards)
Materials: cotton and wool
Turning: varied to achieve different widths between the fence posts
Flowers (24 cards)
Materials: linen and rayon bouclé
Turning: four counterclockwise, four clockwise plus one counterclockwise and one clockwise to create the float areas.
The bird perched on the fence was embroidered on the weaving.

BIBLIOGRAPHY

Alexander, Marthamm. *Simple Weaving*. New York: Taplinger Publishing Co., 1969.

Andersen, Paulli. *Brikvaevning*. Borgen, Denmark.

Atwater, Mary Meigs. *Byways in Handweaving*. New York: Macmillan, 1954.

——. *Notes on Card Weaving*. New York: Universal School of Handicrafts, 1944.

Cox, Doris, and Warren, Barbara. *Creative Hands*. New York: John Wiley & Sons, 1951.

Crowfoot, Grace M. "The Tablet-woven Braids from the Vestments of St. Cuthbert at Durham." *The Antiquaries Journal,* pp. 57-80, vol. XIX, 1938.

——. and Roth, H. Ling. "Were the Ancient Egyptians Conversant with Tablet Weaving (Brettchenweberei, Tissage aux Carton)?" In *Annals of Archaeology and Anthropology*. Liverpool, England: The University Press vol. x nos. 1-2, May 1923.

Tablet Weaving. The Dryad Leaflet III. Leicester, England.

Groff, Russell E. *Cardweaving or Tablet Weaving*. McMinnville, Oregon: Robin and Russ Handweavers, 1969.

Ickis, Marguerite, and Esh, Reba S. *Book of Arts and Crafts*. New York: Dover Press, 1965.

Peach, Mabel. *Tablet Weaving*. Leicester, England: Dryad Handicrafts, 1927.

Pralle, Heinrich. *Tablet Weaving: An Old Peasant Craft*. Hamburg: Kunstgewerbe Schule. Translated by M. and H. H. Peach. Leicester, England: Dryad Works, Handicraft Dept., 1920.

Van Jennet, Arnold, and Jéquier, G. *Le Tissage aux Carton et Son Utilisation Décorative dans l'Egypte Ancienne*. Neuchâtel, Switzerland: DeLachaux & Niestle, 1916.

Zechlin, Ruth. *The Complete Book of Handcrafts*. Amsterdam: Internationale Uitgevery Duphare, 1959.

SUPPLY SOURCES

Casa de las Tejedoras *1619 East Edinger* *Santa Ana, California 92705*	4-holed cards yarns (no samples)
Creative Handweavers *3824 Sunset Boulevard* *Los Angeles, California 90026*	4-holed cards yarns
Fibre Yarn *840 6th Avenue* *New York, New York 10001*	yarns (rayon slide cord, raffia, soutache, etc.)
P. C. Herwig *264 Clinton Street* *Brooklyn, New York 11201*	4-holed cards yarns
Indian Summer *17 East 55th Street* *Hyde Park, Illinois 60615*	4-holed cards yarns
The Jacobsen *2524 Asbury Street* *Evanston, Illinois 60201*	yarns (samples—specializes in rug yarns also suitable for card weaving)
Lily Mills Co. *Shelby, North Carolina 28150*	4-holed cards yarns
Mary Pendleton Handweavers *P.O. Box 233* *Sedona, Arizona 86336*	4-holed cards yarns
Naturalcraft *2199 Bancroft Way* *Berkeley, California 94704*	3-, 4-, and 6-holed cards yarns
North Shore Handweaving Shop *1807 Central Street* *Evanston, Illinois 60201*	4-holed cards yarns
Robin and Russ Handweavers *533 North Adams Street* *McMinnville, Oregon 97128*	4-holed cards yarns
School Products Co., Inc. *312 East 23rd Street* *New York, New York 10010*	4-holed cards looms
Some Place *2990 Adeline Street (at Ashby)* *Berkeley, California 94703*	4-holed cards (plastic) yarns frame looms for cardweaving
Warp, Woof, and Potpourri *1503 North Lake Avenue* *Pasadena, California 91101*	4-holed cards yarns (no samples)
Yarn Depot *545 Sutter Street* *San Francisco, California 94102*	4-holed cards yarns

INDEX

Page numbers for illustrations are in italics